The Only Writing
Series You'll Ever Need:

# Writing
# Children's Books

Lesley Bolton and Lea Wait

Adams Media
Avon, Massachusetts

Contains portions of material adapted and abridged from *The Everything*® *Guide to Writing
Children's Books* by Lesley Bolton, © 2003 F+W Publications, Inc.

Published by Adams Media,
an F+W Publications Company
57 Littlefield Street, Avon, MA 02322
*www.adamsmedia.com*

ISBN 10: 1-59869-088-4
ISBN 13: 978-1-59869-088-0

Printed in the United States of America.

J  I  H  G  F  E  D  C  B  A

Library of Congress Cataloging-in-Publication Data
Bolton, Lesley.
The only writing series you'll ever need : writing children's books /
Lesley Bolton and Lea Wait.
p.    cm.
Includes index.
ISBN-13: 978-1-59869-088-0
ISBN-10: 1-59869-088-4
1. Children's literature--Authorship. I. Wait, Lea. II. Title.
PN147.5.B66 2007
808.06'8--dc22

2006028142

This publication is designed to provide accurate and authoritative information with regard to the
subject matter covered. It is sold with the understanding that the publisher is not engaged in rendering legal, accounting, or other professional advice. If legal advice or other expert assistance is
required, the services of a competent professional person should be sought.
—From a *Declaration of Principles* jointly adopted by a Committee of the American Bar Association
and a Committee of Publishers and Associations

Many of the designations used by manufacturers and sellers to distinguish their products are claimed
as trademarks. Where those designations appear in this book and Adams Media was aware of a
trademark claim, the designations have been printed with initial capital letters.

This book is available at quantity discounts for bulk purchases.
For information, please call 1-800-289-0963.

# Contents

# Introduction

Do you linger in the children's book areas of libraries and bookstores? Do you imagine reading your children or grandchildren a book you've written? Do you have strong memories of books you loved as a child? Do you wish you could create those memories for new generations of children?

You're not alone. Every year thousands of people dream of having their book for children published.

Every year some of those dreams come true.

Every year dozens of authors hold their first books in their hands, see their books in the windows of local bookstores, and proudly sign copies for their family, friends, and fans.

But few dreams come true without study, planning, and hard work. If your dream is to have your writing for children published, then you've taken the first step by picking up this book. Whether you're a beginner or you've already tried to create a picture book or a chapter book and felt discouraged and overwhelmed by all you needed to know—this is the book for you.

I know. Just a few years ago I was an unpublished author who dreamed, too. I read hundreds of children's books, and I read every article and book I could find about writing for children. But no book covered everything I needed to know, from studying the publishing industry, to understanding different categories of children's books, to actually writing a book, to knowing what marketing skills would be required of me as a published author.

It took me years to learn those things. I read, I wrote, and I wrote again. And in 2001 I was one of those first-time authors who proudly held my first book in my hands. Since then I've had three other books for children published. All four have been critically acclaimed and recommended by groups throughout the country. And I'm still writing.

But it might not have taken as long for me to get my first book published if I'd had a book like this one; a book that, in one volume, covers the basics of everything a writer needs to know to get his or her book for children published.

If your dream is to write for children and to have that writing published, and if you're willing to work for that dream, then keep reading. This book may be the beginning of a wonderful journey for you.

A journey that will take your writing to thousands of children who will read your books, and make your stories a part of their life.

Happy reading—and happy writing! May your dreams be filled with happy endings.

Lea Wait

# Chapter 1

# The History and Importance of Children's Books

No one can argue the importance of a child learning to read, think, and communicate, so how could anyone argue the importance of books for children? While books help a child to develop these skills, there are several other reasons that books written and designed specifically for children are important.

## A Brief History of Children's Books

Though children's books are hot items today, this has not always been the case. We take for granted the accessibility of books. Books can be checked out for free at libraries, are prevalent in schools, and can be borrowed from friends and family. For those who want their own, books can be bought anywhere from bookstores to kiosks to grocery stores. Most important, books are readily available to children.

To truly appreciate literature for children, it helps to have an idea of the history of children's books and the steps that were taken to make books appealing to children. However, as a writer, you first need to go even further back and study the art of storytelling through oral tradition.

## Oral Tradition

Before books were available to the common person, storytelling was an oral tradition—and still is in some cultures today. The art of storytelling was highly regarded (even as a profession at times), and stories were passed down to children from their parents, traveling bards, and elders of the community or tribe.

Every culture has used the story to pass on traditions and beliefs to future generations, as well as to explain the mysteries of nature, convey history, set moral standards, influence values, and simply entertain. The spoken word was powerful, and this remains true today.

Storytelling was by no means an easy task. Because the tales told had such a powerful influence and were so important to the culture, they had to be told in such a way that they would not soon be forgotten. Even stories involving war and desperation had to have an entertaining quality that would help the listener to remember so the story could be passed on to future generations. Storytellers often performed their stories and sometimes brought along drawings to help illustrate the tale. Occasionally, they would be forced to embellish or alter a common story to keep the attention of the audience.

Storytellers required a certain knack for sizing up an audience. They had to recognize the needs and wants of those listening and figure out a suitable approach. They also had to alter their techniques according to the type of audience, whether it be adults only, children only, adults and children combined, or people of a different community, town, or tribe. All these factors had to be considered before a story was told.

It is important to recognize and respect the oral tradition. Though commonly thought a thing of the past, it is valuable to the writers of today—especially authors of children's books. As you progress in your writing, you will find that having an audience will help to tone your skills as a storyteller. And just as the storytellers of so long ago had to size up the audience, so will you.

## Modern Books

Though books have been around for quite some time now, books made especially for children have not. Sure, children have had access to books as long as adults have, but there was a very limited selection. In fact, before the seventeenth century, most of the literature children could get their hands on was published for adults. And even if children did choose to struggle through adult texts, what they were allowed to read was riddled with restrictions. Because books had the power to teach and influence, they were somewhat feared; therefore, only those books deemed appropriate in regard to value, morals, and religious beliefs were available to children.

Of course there were a few books made for children before the seventeenth century, such as *The Book of Curtesye* by William Caxton (published in 1477). However, such books were usually instructional and meant to teach a child good manners and behavior. You can imagine what delight the seventeenth century brought when the first books made specifically for the enjoyment of children were produced. For example, *A Book for Boys and Girls; or Country Rhymes for Children* (published in 1686) by John Bunyan was a book designed simply to amuse children.

Though progress was being made in children's literature, the true turning point came about when John Newbery published *A Little Pretty Pocket Book* in 1744. This was the first of several books that were able to combine elements of education and instruction with amusement and entertainment. Newbery's books reached the heights of popularity and soon other publishers began to follow suit.

The nineteenth century brought about a flowering of illustrators, and new printing capabilities allowed for color illustrations to be included in children's books. In America, Scribners published a magazine that was designed specifically for children called *St. Nicholas Magazine*. With the success of this magazine and the quality of writers it attracted, children's publishing began to make its mark.

Soon thereafter, librarians began building collections of children's books; however, they were not satisfied with what was available. They set out on a mission to persuade publishers that there was a market for quality books with illustrations that would appeal to children. Their dedication paid off and in 1921 Macmillan opened the first department solely for trade children's books. Other publishers opened their own departments once it was determined that children's publishing was a profitable enterprise.

Children's publishing snowballed. Certainly the twentieth century pushed the boundaries of what was acceptable and new genres were established. High standards were set and met. This is an exciting time to be involved in children's publishing, whether as an editor, author, or illustrator. Children's publishing is big business and there is a huge market of eager children (and their parents) out there just waiting to be satisfied.

## The Mission and Additional Benefits

There are a number of reasons people write for children. Every person has his or her own story to tell. However, the purpose of children's books—at the most rudimentary level—can be divided into two groups: to teach or to entertain. Of course, oftentimes these two groups intertwine and outstanding books are produced. However, normally the initial idea is rooted in one of the two.

### To Teach

Whether they know it or not, children are hungry for knowledge. Their capacity for learning is tremendous. Several children's authors take advantage of this and set out on a mission to help educate children about topics they feel are important.

In the past, children's books were primarily produced to teach manners and good behavior, to inform children about their culture's present and past, or to school children in religious beliefs and actions appropriate for those beliefs. Some taught lessons in morals and values, while others were straightforward instructional guides pertaining to a particular action. However, this has all changed. While these types of books still exist, the variety of topics available to children has expanded considerably.

Nowadays, books are often designed to help children see what lies outside their own worlds and understand what's happening within them. You can easily find books that teach children about racism, sexuality, war, disease, divorce, and death. Of course there are also books about love, friendship, peace, and strength. With the thousands of topics available, children can discover for themselves where their interests lie. And hopefully one topic of interest will lead to another, which will lead to another, and so forth.

Writers and publishers recognize that it is important to arm children with knowledge. The more they know, the better chance they stand of growing into well-rounded, successful, and happy adults.

### To Entertain

Although books intended to teach a valuable lesson are well and good, everyone needs a little fun—especially kids. If you haven't noticed, children can have a very short attention span. Children are usually straightforward and honest (especially when it comes to their likes and dislikes), and don't have to bend to niceties as adults often do. If a child is bored, he or she will let you know. A good children's book can make all the difference between a squirming child and an attentive child.

Some children's books are designed solely to entertain or amuse. Often these books will have a rhyming or otherwise lulling language that amuses, calms, or comforts a child. Sometimes they are used to divert a child's attention from a disappointment, such as not being able to play outside while it's raining. They will keep a child busy having fun in not-so-fun places such as the doctor's office. And let's not forget, some are just meant to tell a good story.

For those who argue that books designed solely for entertainment have no value, think again. If those books grab the attention of a child and spark an interest in reading, what greater value is there? There are several different types of books, and entertainment, whether on its own or combined with instruction, is an important quality that children's books possess.

### Other Benefits

Supplementing the purposes of teaching and entertaining, children's books are loaded with additional benefits. While these benefits may not be as blatant as their overall purpose, as a writer, you should be aware of the impact your book may have. Also, to be aware of these underlying influences may help to motivate you when you reach that point in every writer's life when you throw your hands in the air and ask, "Why do I bother?"

Perhaps the most important benefit of a book is promoting literacy. Let's face it, those who are able to read and write have an easier go of things in this world than those who are illiterate. Every book, whether or not it was designed specifically for this purpose, can help a child to grasp language and literacy. If a child is able to derive pleasure and perhaps satisfy a curiosity from a book at a young age, that child is more likely to make books a part of his or her life. Those who read extensively are quite often good writers, have a strong vocabulary, are able to express themselves and communicate effectively, and have sound grammar and spelling skills.

## Helpful Hints

Books can help continuously inspire and promote creativity. By introducing new ideas, a book will stimulate the mind to go off on tangents, creating a cycle of original thought.

Listening is hard—even adults have difficulty with it. Listening is different from hearing. It is a very important skill that takes practice and patience. While hearing is simply the process of registering sound through the ear, listening requires active participation in comprehending what is being heard. Children will develop good listening skills if they are read to on a regular basis, especially if started off at a very young age. By helping to strengthen their listening skills, you are also helping them to become better communicators.

If you've ever had contact with children, you know that they are naturally creative and can sometimes have wild imaginations. Since it seems like just part of their charm, many take their creativity for granted. As children grow older, outside influences can stifle creativity, and they can find themselves as adults wondering where their imagination fled to.

Just like adults, children sometimes need a form of escapism to take a breather from the trials of life. Children are very perceptive and can feel the strain of tense situations even if they are not able to fully express these feelings. With all of the harmful forms of escapism available to children today, books should be made available as a healthy choice for distraction. Books can transport the reader to a different time and place, leaving behind the present and all its troubles.

## A Child's World

It is important to realize that children's books are most often bought by adults. Because you will want your books to appeal to an adult's sensibility, it is sometimes easy to allow yourself to be swayed by an adult's viewpoint when writing. What you must keep in mind is that ultimately children's books are for children, regardless of who buys them. It is this quality that makes books so important to the children themselves. Books can become a secret treasure. Children can explore their own tastes and interests through the books they choose to read. If they feel as though a book was written and designed just for them, children will create a bond with the literature. So, write children's books for children.

To write successfully for children, you need to acknowledge their view of the world, which can be quite different from that of an adult.

You don't need a degree in child psychology to understand children. You have two excellent resources at your fingertips: your memories and children themselves. We'll get into the specifics of writing for children later in the book. For right now, get to know them.

### Use Your Memory

Somewhere in the back of your mind, you know what it is to be a child. Though that may seem like ages ago, it is there locked in your memory. If you can get in touch with your inner child, it will help you write for children.

If you are having difficulty remembering specifics from your childhood, start off with a description of yourself. Pick a particular age that you can see most clearly. Sketch out a brief character description including things such as your age, hair color, eye color, height, weight, clothing preferences, hobbies, friends, where you lived, and general likes and dislikes. This will help you to gain a sense of self. The more details you can remember, the better.

## Helpful Hints

Try looking at some pictures of you as a child. A picture can say a thousand words and even trigger some memories that you may have forgotten!

Next, write down a timeline of significant events during your childhood. Leave some room between each because one memory may spark another and you might want to go back and add something. Once you are satisfied with your timeline, take each event individually and retell the story in first person—but try to tell it as you would have immediately following its occurrence. Use the character description to get you going; how old were you and what did you look like during this event? Then go on to describe how you felt, what your reactions were, and what you observed. Complete this exercise for each event. You will probably find that the more stories you retell, the easier they are to describe from a child's point of view.

A child's view is quite different from that of an adult. For one thing, a child is short. Therefore, what is in his or her direct line of vision is going to be different from that of a six-foot man. Also, a child's priorities differ from an adult's. While a security blanket may be the most important thing in the world to a child, an adult may look at it as just another piece of cloth. As you try to recapture this view, take these observations into consideration and use your own memories to help gain a better understanding of children and their world.

### Go 007!

One of the best ways to get to know children is to watch them. If you have children of your own, this is a great place to start, but don't limit yourself to a select few. (Plus, your own children will most likely take more notice of your presence, and their behavior may be influenced by it.) If at all possible, study large groups of children. Pay close attention to what they say, how they interact with each other and adults, what they take interest in, and their body language.

## Helpful Hints

In this day and age, it is considered very inappropriate for an adult to sit in a playground or park and observe children. As innocent as your intentions are, you could still be perceived as a threat to the children by parents or teachers. Don't sit and watch—get involved with some volunteering!

Don't hesitate to volunteer at schools, churches, or any other groups to interact and observe children. This will give you the opportunity to see how children behave, plus it's rewarding—and fun!

Keep a notebook with you and jot down your observations, even if they don't seem to have any significance. If you hear conversations, write them down word for word—it just may help you with dialogue when it comes time to write your story.

If you are unable to observe children firsthand or would like additional resources, you may want to consider reading books and magazines on parenting. These references will help you to understand the physical and emotional milestones and conduct of a child's growth process, especially babies and toddlers.

## Not Just Books

Children's books are important for reading purposes of course, but they also inspire movies and television shows. This can be good and it can be bad, depending on how you choose to look at it. On the one hand, blockbuster movies and hit television series will raise awareness of the book. As an author, you will be able to reach a wider audience—both the children who have already read your book and those who haven't. On the other hand, because these adaptations are not books, the producers will usually need to alter the story somewhat to either make the story fit within a specific time allotment or appeal to a more diverse audience. Those children who see the story acted out for them may not bother reading the book, but then there are also those children who love the story so much, they beg their parents to take them to the bookstore immediately. It works both ways.

### Helpful Hints

Using the Internet can help, too! Surf the Net to find some blogs written by children's authors, or even some Web sites that kids regularly visit.

Think about your favorite children's movies. Are any of these based on books? What about television series? For instance, Laura Ingalls Wilder wrote a series of books that was later adapted into the *Little House on the Prairie* television series. *Black Beauty* was turned into a movie and touched the hearts of thousands of children. *Anne of Green Gables* was made into a movie and a television series. These are just three examples; there are hundreds, perhaps thousands, out there. Take a look at some of today's popular children's movies and television shows. You will probably be surprised at the number of them that are based on books.

While Walt Disney has Mickey and friends as a huge attraction, you can't escape those characters from famous fairy tales—Snow White, Cinderella, Sleeping Beauty, Beauty and the Beast, and so on. Walt Disney knew what he was doing when he brought to life these famous fairy tales in movie form. The movies themselves are considered classics. However, they would not exist had the stories not been first written down for children.

Quality children's books are important not just to those children who are eager readers, but also to those children who prefer to have stories performed for them.

## Technological Advancements

Some people are of the opinion that advancements in technology are going to cause the extinction of the book. This fear is not new and has pushed the panic buttons of publishers and writers alike with the emergence of new technologies such as television, videos, video games, computers, and the Internet. However, the children's book has stood its ground throughout all these new breakthroughs in entertainment.

The new buzz of publishing technology today is the e-book, or electronic book. An e-book is simply a book that is set in an electronic format. These books must be read using a computer or handheld electronic viewer. While e-books are available today and the market is preparing for expansion, it is still in its infancy. Printed books are still very popular and there is no cause for alarm—yet. It will take quite some time for the e-book to worm its way into the hearts of readers.

People still have a close relationship with printed books. The ability to scribble in the margins, highlight passages, dog-ear pages, and feel the paper between your fingers as you build the anticipation of turning the page are sentimental qualities that aren't soon to be forgotten. How many times have you opened a new book and took a big whiff? How many times have you scanned someone's bookshelf for something good to read and picked out a book that was well worn? How often have you taken a great book into a bubble bath with you? The printed book is going to be around for a long time.

# Chapter 2

# Different Types of Children's Books

Because the classification of children's books spans such a wide age and reading-level range—infants to teenagers—there have to be distinct divisions that break it down into smaller categories. For example, a novel appropriate for a young adult is most likely not going to capture the attention of a six-year-old. This chapter will outline the different formats of children's books.

## The Standards

The two standard categories of books are fiction and nonfiction, plus a hybrid called faction. Simply put, fiction is made up and nonfiction is fact; faction is a combination. However, these categories are broad and allow a lot of room for creativity within them. Think of them as umbrellas for every type of book. Before you begin writing, you will need to decide if you are going to write fiction, nonfiction, or faction. From there, you will then decide which type of children's book and reading level best suit both you and your story.

### Fiction

Most people first think of fiction when they think of children's books. Fiction seems to be limited only by the extent of your imagination. At the heart of fiction is a story; at the heart of nonfiction is fact.

Fiction comes in several different forms: fairy tales, legends, folk tales, myths, romantic fiction, historical fiction, fantasy, ghost stories, science fiction, westerns, adventure stories, and horror, to name a few. But you don't have to imitate books in these genres. As long as you have combined a little bit of imagination with all the components of a story, you have a work of fiction.

The fantasy doesn't have to end with just the storyline. Even the choice of characters is left up to your own imagination. A character can be as far-fetched as an alien from the planet Zanatov or as down-to-earth as a mother. Perhaps you would like to explore what it is to be an animal and give an animal the lead role in your story, complete with voice, clothes, job, and family. Or maybe you would like to explore life after death and characterize a ghost or spirit.

## Helpful Hints

Don't let the freedom of fiction interfere with telling a good story. If everything that happens in your story is wild and not of this world, children will have difficulty relating to it.

The setting for your story can be a work of pure fiction as well. Maybe that alien is quite partial to his home of Zanatov and doesn't even bother visiting Earth. Perhaps your character is lost in a small remote region of a jungle. Or if you've dreamed of a castle beneath the sea, make that dream come to life in the form of a story.

Fiction can also have a basis in fact. You needn't suffer under the pressure of inventing everything in your story. If it helps your story, feel free to touch it up with a bit of reality, truth, or fact. Because it isn't entirely factual, it is still considered fiction even though it has specks of truth. (This is called faction, but we'll get to that in a moment.)

## Nonfiction

Nonfiction is factual or reference material. Even though nonfiction must abide by the truth and stick to the cold hard facts, it isn't nearly as boring as it sounds. Writing nonfiction for children requires a lot of creativity. As a writer, you must find a way to make these facts appealing to children.

Though you may believe that nonfiction is rather limited by its requirement of truth, it actually offers just as many opportunities as fiction. Nonfiction books cover a wide range of already established topics and new discoveries are being made every day. Science, history, geography, nature, cooking, biography, evolution, and disease are just a few of the topics that can be explored in children's books.

In addition to the endless topics available, there are also different approaches you can take to present the topic. For example, nearly any activity can be transformed into a how-to book. Or perhaps you are full of useless but amusing trivia and decide to make a compilation of little-known facts. Maybe you would like to create a documentary-style book about the Pony Express. Find something that interests you that you think will interest children as well.

## Helpful Hints

Get creative (though not so creative that you start making stuff up!) with your subject matter and make sure the text is lively. Remember that your readers are children, and you should write about a nonfiction topic in a way that keeps their interest—but doesn't stretch the truth to do it.

If you believe you would like to write nonfiction, think about your own activities and interests. What is your occupation? Where did you grow up? Is there a subject you'd like to learn more about? What are your hobbies? Use the answers to these questions as starting points for your compilation of ideas.

**Faction**

Faction is a combination of fiction and nonfiction. Essentially, it falls within the fiction category simply because it is not entirely factual; however, having a basis in fact, it isn't entirely fiction either. Faction is a wonderful area that can help enliven and dramatize a factual account or help to make a fantasy convincing.

Have you ever watched a movie or television show that was "based on a true story"? Perhaps the story itself isn't quite dramatic or thrilling enough to capture an audience, but with a little added flair, it becomes a blockbuster hit. This is a common example of faction.

## Helpful Hints

Sometimes an interesting idea is to insert real historical figures into the story as side characters who appear only once or very rarely. For example, if you write a children's book set in American Revolution-era New England, your main character could see or interact briefly with some historical figures from that period.

You can create faction by adding fiction to fact. Oftentimes, it is a simple fact that ignites the imagination, creating a wonderful storyline. For example, let's say you are a history buff and are fascinated with the Civil War. Obviously, you don't know firsthand what it was like to live during that war, but your imagination can take the facts and run with them. Write a story in first person and let your mind's eye recreate the war with you in the midst of it.

Another way to create faction is to add fact to fiction. Perhaps you have an excellent story set in a faraway land you have never visited. Facts about the foreign land would help to give the story a realistic feel, even if the story itself is pure fantasy. You could use facts about the natural environment to complement the setting, or perhaps even introduce a native of the land as a character.

Once you decide whether you want to write fiction, nonfiction, or faction, you need to decide what you want your book to look like and what reading level you want to address. Let's take a look at other types of children's books and the reading levels appropriate to each one.

## Picture Books

When speaking of children's books, most people first think of picture books. These are the books that combine illustrations with text. They are the books that are read at bedtime, during story hour at the library, in kindergarten classes, and by older siblings to younger ones. They mark the beginning of a child's knowledge of literature.

At most bookstores, picture books take up a good portion of the children's department. They are popular with both children and adults. Kids browse the bookshelves looking at the lively illustrations and stunning colors. Parents browse the bookshelves looking for a story that will be a pleasure to read over and over again to their children. Some adults love to give picture books as gifts—to people of all ages.

### The Design

Picture books are probably the most structured of all children's books. They are normally between twenty-four and thirty-two pages long. While you may think that is plenty of space to tell your story, these page counts include the front matter (copyright page, title page, dedication, acknowledgment, and any other information pages). For example, a thirty-two-page picture book minus the front matter may leave only twenty-eight pages for the story.

### Helpful Hints

Word counts for picture books normally range between 200 and 1,500 words. There are exceptions. Some picture books have very small illustrations, leaving room for a lot of text. Others have no words at all.

To help you write within the structure of picture books, try breaking up your text into pages. The first page of your story will normally be on the right-hand page, so it will stand alone. Pages 2 and 3 will be a two-page spread so a small cliffhanger should occur on the odd-numbered pages throughout.

Also, you will want to envision the illustrations that may accompany your text. You shouldn't state anything in your text that can be understood in the illustration. Enough action in the text should take place on each page to allow for an illustration. On the other hand, you don't want too much action because there might not be room to illustrate it all. Writing picture books is a very delicate and time-consuming process; however, if you aren't frightened off, it is also a very rewarding experience.

### Writing Picture Books

First of all, let's do away with a common misconception: You do not have to be able to illustrate to write and sell picture books. And unless you are a professional illustrator, do not submit drawings with your text.

While picture books are easy to read and love, they are not easy to write. Yes, the text may be quite simple and short, but that is misleading. Because space is limited in picture books, every single word must be very carefully chosen; you simply don't have the room to take your time with the story. Plus, the writer must take into consideration the illustrations.

Children typically have a short attention span. If you want to capture their interest, your text should be constantly moving. Every page should contain action, including the very first page. Don't spend precious space setting up the story; just dive right in there. You want to capture the child's attention from the get-go. Plus, you'll keep their attention by including small cliffhangers that motivate them to turn the page. Just as novels leave you wanting to read more with the end of each chapter, picture books leave you with that desire at the end of each spread.

If you want to write picture books, spend some time at a bookstore or library and take a look at the structure and style of the picture books available. Ask the librarian or salesperson which picture books are popular and look closely at these. Also, spend time with books that seem boring or unappealing and try to pinpoint why you don't like them. The more time you can spend in the current children's book market, the better you will get to know what does and does not work.

### Types of Picture Books

When you browse the bookshelves for picture books, you'll notice that there are several different types. The most common has a large illustration accompanied by a few lines of text on each page. But not every story works best in this format. Therefore, other types of picture books are available:

- **Board or baby books.** These books are built to stand up to the destructive tendencies of babies and toddlers. They are often made of cardboard and are usually sixteen pages long with an illustration accompanied by only a couple of words per page.
- **Wordless picture books.** Just as the name implies, these picture books do not have text. The illustrations tell the story by themselves.
- **Novelty books.** These books have an additional element that makes the book interactive or otherwise entertaining. Some novelty books have pop-ups, pull tabs, graduated page lengths, holes in the pages, or accessories that complement the story.
- **Concept books.** These books focus on one concept and don't necessarily have to tell a story. Whether they are about colors or overcoming a fear of the dark, concept books explore a concept in whatever format suits it best.

**Examples of Picture Books**

*Where the Wild Things Are* by Maurice Sendak
*Goodnight Moon* by Margaret Wise Brown
*The Snowy Day* by Ezra Jack Keats
*Blueberries for Sal* by Robert McCloskey
*Corduroy* by Don Freeman
*The Velveteen Rabbit* by Margery Williams
*The Tale of Peter Rabbit* by Beatrix Potter

# Early Readers

Children learning to read may start off with picture books, often because that is what they are accustomed to and that's what is lying around the house. However, as they progress, their self-confidence is heightened. They are proud of their "big kid" abilities and start to look down on "baby books." This is where early readers step in.

Because children learn so quickly, not much time is spent in this transitional phase of reading. However, this does not diminish the importance of early readers. These books are valuable stepping stones that will promote a child's enthusiasm and comprehension.

## The Design

Early readers are books designed specifically for children who are learning to read. The books are usually taller and not as wide as picture books. They have a more grown-up, sophisticated feel that children love. But they aren't so sophisticated that they overwhelm a child. The books normally use large type and the spacing between the lines is increased to allow for more white space on a page.

## Helpful Hints

These books vary in page lengths and word counts. Typically an early reader is forty-eight to sixty-four pages long, with some of the simpler books being thirty-two pages. The word counts are comparable to picture books, though they normally shoot for the higher end of around 1,500 words.

Although not classified as picture books, early readers do have illustrations. Whereas picture books rely on the illustrations to help the viewer capture the story, early readers focus on the words to secure the story, using illustrations to provide prompts for the reader while enhancing the entertainment.

### Writing Early-Reader Books

When writing early readers you must keep in mind that while they are for older children, the text can't be as complex as some picture books. Picture books are most often read by adults to children and can make use of an extended vocabulary and sentence structure. Although early readers should have simple text, this does not mean that you should avoid big words. Children are smart and crave knowledge. If you fill an early reader with very straightforward and uncomplicated words, a child will feel his or her intelligence is insulted.

Don't be afraid to throw in a big word here and there if it helps promote the story. However, if you do use a word that children may not have heard before, try to use it again somewhere in the story. Of course you don't want to go overboard and have that same word on every page, nor do you want to riddle the story with complicated vocabulary. Find a good balance that will help a child to learn but not frustrate and discourage him or her.

While early readers can help strengthen a child's vocabulary, this is not the time or place to delve into advanced sentence structures. Keep the sentences simple and concise. Short and snappy text will give the book a rhythm and progression that a child can handle.

The plot, also, must be simple. Use a single, uncomplicated concept or problem and focus on its development, avoiding unnecessary detail. Like picture books, the story must be constantly moving. Use action, dialogue, and rich language to keep the story going. If you allow the story to idle for too long, a child will get bored and put down the book. Children can be unmerciful critics, and if you don't keep their attention at all times, you can lose their favor.

**Examples of Early-Reader Books**

*Are You My Mother?* by P. D. Eastman

*The Cat in the Hat* by Dr. Seuss

*Little Bear* by Else Holmelund Minarik

*Chester* by Syd Hoff

*Frog and Toad* series by Arnold Lobel

*Arthur's Prize Reader* by Lillian Hoban

# Chapter Books

Chapter books are the next step up for a developing reader. These books welcome those who are getting bored with the early readers and are ready to advance their reading level. A chapter book should be relatively simple in storyline, language, and sentence structure, but it should also be somewhat of a challenge. Again, because children learn so quickly, not a whole lot of time will be spent on chapter books, but these books are important for a child who wants to make a smooth transition to the novel.

## The Design

Chapter books, like early readers, are designed to give the book a "grown-up" feel. While the exterior of the book may look a lot like early readers, the interior is a bit different. Early readers have a lot of white space, which is welcoming to a child just learning to read on his or her own. When the child reaches the level of chapter books, he or she won't be as intimidated by lines of text. Therefore, the text of chapter books is usually a little smaller than that of early readers, and there isn't as much space between lines. Chapter books usually have some illustrations, but the story doesn't rely on them to help the reader along.

The story is broken down into several small chapters, paving the way for longer chapters in middle-grade books. Because these books have more text and generally more pages than early readers, the completion of each chapter gives the child a sense of satisfaction while not pressuring the child to finish the entire book in one sitting.

## Helpful Hints

Chapter books are normally between forty-eight and eighty pages long, though there are certainly those that are longer. Obviously, word counts (between 1,500 and 10,000) are going to be boosted since more text can fit on a page and there are fewer illustrations.

### Writing Chapter Books

When writing chapter books, you should keep the plot simple, focusing on one specific concept or problem. The plots are usually centered on an experience children are familiar with. Children, at this stage in particular, like to relate to the stories they are reading. Using a setting that is recognizable and making the hero or heroine of the story a child are both good ways to capture the interest of your reader.

The story needs to be full of action. Each chapter should include an action episode that helps the story along. Children get restless very easily. Every single sentence should hook the reader and the easiest way to accomplish this is to keep the story moving with action.

Kids love humor. If at all possible, definitely use humor in your story. Because chapter books most often portray common childhood experiences, humor can help a child to make light of situations that might normally be humiliating or grim. However, be careful with your use of humor; you don't want to turn everything into a joke, nor do you want to make fun of children. Keep it light and happy.

Dialogue is also important in chapter books. Using dialogue is a sneaky way of creating white space without the child realizing it. Even though they may consider themselves advanced readers, they will still breathe a sigh of relief when there is a little more white space on the page. Dialogue can be tricky for chapter books. It has to move the story along; children will get bored with everyday exchanges.

Also, the dialogue has to be smooth and natural. A child will easily spot forced dialogue and be turned off by it.

### Examples of Chapter Books
*Sarah, Plain and Tall* by Patricia MacLachlan
*Pippi Longstocking* by Astrid Lindgren
*Ramona the Pest* by Beverly Cleary
*Goosebumps* series by R. L. Stine
*Baby-Sitters Little Sister* series by Ann M. Martin
*The Secret of the Attic* by Sheri Cooper Sinykin

## Middle School

Middle-grade books mark an important milestone in reading development. While picture books, early readers, and chapter books are also significant, they are normally selected for children by adults and often require some dependence on an adult for understanding. Middle-grade books, however, are for the independent reader.

## Helpful Hints

Middle grade books usually run between 80 and 192 pages. Word counts vary between 20,000 and 45,000 words.

During this phase, children are coming into their own. They are discovering their own preferences and interests. They are taking up hobbies and making decisions for themselves. They are becoming more aware of the world and their standing in it. Trends, friends, gender, and personal taste influence their reading selections more so than adults do.

### The Design

Middle-grade novels are divided into chapters that are longer than those in chapter books, but not quite as long as those in young adult books. The text is not quite as dense as that of adult novels, but there isn't a whole lot of white space either. There may be a few illustrations here and there, but not normally more than one per chapter.

### Writing Middle-School Books

The storyline of a middle-grade novel is normally conflict driven. The plot should be clearly defined, and the main character should be someone a child can relate to. Your readers will want to read about characters like themselves and their peers, therefore it is best to try to keep adult characters to a minimum. While including adults will be necessary in some instances, let the main character (a child) solve the problem or handle the conflict. If an adult steps in to save the day, the child loses his or her sense of independence. The main character is important in middle-grade books and should be well developed.

Middle-grade readers can handle detail as long as you don't drown them in it. At this age they want to be able to create a picture in their minds of the characters and setting. Be as specific as possible and work in details naturally. Also, try to stay away from describing everything and everyone in the first chapter. You need to get the story moving as soon as possible, even within the first line. You have time to get to know your characters and the setting.

Tell your story from only one child's perspective. This will not only keep the story from becoming too jumbled, but also help the reader relate to the character.

### Examples of Middle-School Books

*Little House on the Prairie* by Laura Ingalls Wilder
*A Wrinkle in Time* by Madeleine L'Engle
*The Secret Garden* by Frances Hodgson Burnett
*The Indian in the Cupboard* by Lynne Reid Banks
*Black Beauty* by Anna Sewell
*Deliver Us from Evie* by M. E. Kerr

## Young Adult

The young adult category dangles at the edge of the realm of children's books. Because these books are written for a teenage audience (age twelve and older), they aren't quite children's books per se, yet they aren't adult books either. Young adult (YA) books fall within the children's book category because it is normally the children's department of a publishing company or a publishing company that specializes in children's books that publishes them.

## Helpful Hints

Young adult books are written for just that, young adults. They aren't directed at just children, and often target those between the ages of twelve and early twenties. Their length is usually 175 to 300 pages, and word count rounds out at about 40,000 to 75,000 words.

While the term *young adult book* is used frequently in the publishing world, the audience prefers to use teen novel. YA books are relatively new. Before the 1960s, the young adult novel was a book published for adults but suitable for teenagers. Now we have books published specifically for teens with teen issues, teen characters, and teen interests, exploring that chaotic world between childhood and adulthood.

### Writing YA Books

The teen years are times of trial, pressure, questions, ups and downs, self-consciousness, and drama. As an adult writing for teens, you must try to recapture that tumultuous time. Even though teens may be dealing with adult issues, their priorities and outlooks differ from an adult's. As if teenagers don't have enough to worry about with adult issues, they have their own issues as well. You are free to explore almost any topic in YA books, but if you want to get published, make sure it is in good taste.

Try to remember how you felt as a teenager. What was the most important thing to you at that time? What motivated you? What did you worry about? What tough decisions did you have to make? What kind of pressures did you have to deal with? What were your friends like? Remembering your own teenage years will help you to relate to the teens of today, but keep in mind that times can change rather quickly. You need to stay abreast of today's trends and issues.

Writing for teenagers may give you more of a sense of freedom than writing for younger children. The story should be challenging and thought-provoking. The average teen has a strong vocabulary and can handle complex sentence structures. And because YA books are longer than other children's books, you have more room in which to tell your story.

### Examples of YA Books

*To Kill a Mockingbird* by Harper Lee
*The Catcher in the Rye* by J. D. Salinger
*The Outsiders* by S. E. Hinton
*Animal Farm* by George Orwell
*The Hobbit* by J. R. R. Tolkien
*Of Mice and Men* by John Steinbeck

# Chapter 3

# Do You Have It in You?

Though you may have toyed with the idea of becoming a children's book author and possibly have written a few stories already, if you are serious about wanting to break into the field, you need to first determine your motives and goals. This chapter will help you determine whether you have what it takes to become a children's writer.

## What Are Your Motives?

Children's books don't just appear out of thin air. A lot of hard work, time, and thought goes into each and every one. So what motivates writers to dedicate themselves and put so much work into a book? Everyone has his or her own reasons. What are yours?

If you want to contribute to the world of children's literature, you first need to figure out why. Your reasons and sources of motivation will affect your writing, even if only in the smallest way. You need to be aware of this before you can take an objective look at your work.

### Fame and Fortune

If you think writing children's books is a quick way to travel down that road to fame and fortune, think again. Though the media may glamorize the life of an author with whirlwind book tours, fancy houses, and limousine service, this isn't the typical life of an author. Go to a library or bookstore and take a look around. How many books do you see? Now how many authors do you hear about in the media? The numbers don't equate.

This isn't to say that you won't be one of the lucky few who do reach fame and fortune; it just means that you shouldn't let this be your driving force. If money provides an incentive to get to work, that's fine. But you should probably have other motivations spurring you on as well if you hope to be happy in writing for children.

Writing solely to gain fame and fortune will affect what you write. You will most likely be influenced by the media and the trends they push. If you are able to catch a trend and ride it with your work, you will probably make a pretty penny. However, catching a trend in the publishing industry is a difficult thing to do. The book you write will take one to three years to reach the shelves from the original idea. As you well know, trends are often short-lived and pass by quickly. What was hot yesterday could be lame today.

### Passion

Some people write because they have to. It is more than a hobby; it is a way of life. They find satisfaction in sitting down at the computer or typewriter every day simply to express themselves. Writing can be very therapeutic and a lot of fun. These people probably aren't too concerned about getting published and reaching a wide audience. Most likely they write for themselves only.

### Helpful Hints

Those who are driven by passion and self-expression are very close to their work. If you fall into this category, you should be aware that while loving your work is a good thing, you might sometimes find it difficult to accept criticism. Criticism will be a part of your publishing experience, and you will have to learn to accept criticism of your work and not take it as a personal insult.

Once your book is finished and you send it to editors or literary agents, it is no longer nestled in the safety of your keeping. Agents and editors may view your work in a different light. They may have suggestions for improvement or flat-out reject it. While this can be discouraging, you should learn from it and move on. Try to take a step back and look at your work objectively. Don't give up!

### To Teach

Some people set out to become authors of children's books because they want to communicate with a wide audience of children. They feel they have something important to say or teach, and they want to influence and inspire children. This is an admirable reason to write children's books, but like the other motives we've just mentioned, it can affect the quality, style, and/or strength of your work.

## Helpful Hints

As a children's book author, there are some basic tools that you will need:

- Computer with printer and Internet access
- Unabridged dictionary with thesaurus
- *Chicago Manual of Style* and Strunk and White's *Elements of Style*
- Library card

When you feel very strongly about a message you want to convey, sometimes your fervor can stand in the way of your storytelling technique and abilities. Perhaps you become so caught up in the importance of the message that you fail to make the book entertaining. Or maybe you do make the story entertaining but are so worried that the kids won't get the message that you reiterate it constantly.

This isn't to say that you should sugarcoat issues. Children are aware of the problems in today's world. If you want to communicate an issue or message to a child, have the characters in your story explore the issue. Allow the characters to suffer consequences of actions, but also allow the characters to figure out and solve the problem. Try to write a story in which you convey the message through dramatization, humor, exaggeration, or point of view.

## Tools of the Trade

At the very least, all you really have to have to write children's books is a writing utensil and something to write on. However, if you want to make it to publication, there are a few other tools that will help you along the way. Don't forget that the children's publishing world is very competitive, and you will stand a better chance of success if you tap every resource.

### Are You Computer Savvy?

Because most editors do not accept handwritten manuscripts, you will need a computer or word processor. If you do not already own one and can't justify the expense at the moment, don't fret. Chances are you have a friend or relative with a computer, and even if you don't, you can still gain access at libraries or stores that rent time on computers.

If you are serious about writing, you will eventually need to get a computer of your own. There are some great deals on the market. Plus, people are constantly upgrading their own systems and selling their older, perfectly competent machines. Just make sure that the computer has word processing capabilities.

Along with the computer, you will want to get a printer. While it is becoming common to e-mail manuscripts to editors, you should have a hard copy of your work. Some editors even work entirely off hard copy, though these are few and far between.

Internet access provides a wonderful helping hand to both aspiring and seasoned writers. You will need to do research on the market, and on publishing companies, and for the story itself in most cases. The Internet has a wealth of information readily available. Using the Internet could easily cut the time spent researching at libraries. Plus, the Internet offers several Web sites, message boards, and chat rooms dedicated to children's writing, which may be able to answer some of your questions and help you with the writing process.

Once you have Internet access, you will want to get an e-mail account. E-mail has become an accepted, and often preferred, way of communicating. Editors find that e-mail is less time-consuming than telephone calls or letters. Plus, some editors accept manuscripts via e-mail, which cuts down on the time and cost of sending your manuscript via snail mail.

If you aren't accustomed to using a computer, don't be intimidated. Word processing programs are quite easy to use. You may want to consider taking a class or seminar. Or perhaps you have a friend or relative willing to help you get started. You will learn a lot on your own simply by playing around with it and trying out its different features.

### References You Need to Know

There are several reference books you will want to have on hand to take you through the writing process. While it isn't necessary to own these books to write a good story, if you want to present a clean manuscript to an editor, they will certainly come in handy. You can always visit the reference section of a library to get access to these books; however, you will find that building your own library will save you time and energy, because you will probably refer to these books often.

First of all, you need a comprehensive and up-to-date dictionary. The pocket dictionaries will not do. There is a certain comfort in seeing a large, hardbound, complete dictionary and knowing that thousands of words are available to you. The simple pocket dictionaries are lacking in many words, and quite often it is those words you need to look up.

Almost hand in hand with a dictionary is a thesaurus. Again, you need one of the comprehensive hardbound editions. While you may be accustomed to using the thesaurus on your word processing system, you will find it can't compare to a quality book.

*The Chicago Manual of Style* is used consistently by publishing houses. This book pretty much sets the standard for style in the publishing world. Of course, individual companies will have their own style, but this is usually in conjunction with the *Chicago Manual of Style*. Be sure to get the most recent edition.

Another great little book to refer to for style and grammar is Strunk and White's *Elements of Style*. If you have ever taken a writing class, you probably already own this. It is a small and concise book that reviews the rules of style, punctuation, and grammar.

## Dedication and Space

Not only will you need to dedicate time to writing, but you will also need to dedicate space. If you want to do your best, you will need to concentrate solely on your work, at least for specified periods of time. This is best accomplished by dedicating a particular area of your home to a workstation for your writing.

### Helpful Hints

Once you pick out and set up your workspace, try to stay out of it unless you are working. Try to make sure your workspace is not at the center of traffic in your home and you can easily not see or pass it. That way you'll subconsciously associate the space with your writing and nothing else.

If you have a spare room or study, the task will be an easy one. However, if you don't have that extra rarely used space, you will just have to get creative. Maybe you have an attic or basement that could easily be turned into a small home office. If not, take a good look at the space available in the other rooms of your house. Do your children have a playroom? Perhaps you could work in there while the children are at school or after they have gone to bed.

Look for the least used areas of the house. Setting up a workstation in the living room may not be such a great idea if the rest of your family spends most of their time there. (You also wouldn't want the added distraction or temptation of the television.) Do you have a dining room that is used only in the evenings? Or maybe you could rearrange your bedroom furniture and designate a corner of the room as your workstation.

Once you have chosen an area, you need to organize it to make the best use of the space. At the very least, you will need a desk and good lighting. You may also want to make room for a filing cabinet and bookcase. You will want all of your reference materials within reach so you don't waste time and concentration getting up and walking across the room for needed materials.

If your family is home during your scheduled writing time, talk to them and stress how important it is that you are not disturbed when you are at your workstation. If you can shut yourself in a room, do. It may be difficult at first, but it is essential that you dedicate time and space to your writing endeavor. It is up to you to make it happen.

## Be Realistic, Now!

If you are serious about writing children's books, it helps to know what you are getting into. At the risk of sounding discouraging, the world of children's publishing is not for everyone. You must be patient, persistent, hardworking, and certainly have a bit of talent.

Children's publishers receive thousands of manuscripts a year and only a small percentage of those make it to print. To be able to compete with and stand out from these thousands of other writers, you have to do tons of research, write and rewrite, open yourself to criticism, and be persistent even in the face of rejection. You have to be willing to devote a lot of time, sometimes even years, to just one book.

### Don't Give Your Two-Week Notice Just Yet

As stated before, children's publishing is not the way to go if you are looking for an overnight fortune. While there are indeed those who have reached fame and fortune with their children's books, the odds are against you. Even if you really believe in your ability to write successfully, now is not the time to quit your current job. You will need the money to survive while you struggle through the obstacles every writer faces.

It often takes writers several years and several published books before they are able to become full-time writers. As a writer you won't receive a steady income that you can predict and rely upon. Writing is hard enough. If you add the stress and pressure of relying on a book to be a moneymaker, your work will be affected and you won't be able to give 100 percent to it.

Let's say that after years of blood, sweat, and tears, you achieve your goal: You are a full-time writer. Certainly you should be thrilled about your success and celebrate appropriately, but after all the party guests have gone, you might find yourself sitting down to a very lonely occupation.

## Helpful Hints

If you made time to write while maintaining a full-time job, you know that peace and quiet are moments to be treasured and taken advantage of. However, if you quit your job to become a full-time writer, you may find that the peace and quiet you once treasured soon becomes a nightmare.

Especially if you have just come from a busy office environment, the silence, broken only by the hum of your computer, can be quite distracting. The lack of human interaction may take its toll on you and affect your work. You may find yourself wanting to do laundry, do the dishes, or even watch talk shows on television—anything other than sitting in the quiet staring at a blank screen.

If you haven't mastered self-discipline, it can be easy to fall behind in your work. Writing is something you have to do on your own; there's really no getting around it. And you have to be able to concentrate while spending several hours alone. You need to take this into consideration before taking the plunge into full-time writing. Knowing what to expect may help to make that transition a little easier. Although this may sound very disheartening, being a full-time writer is a very rewarding experience.

So you've made it through the realistic outlook without backing out. Good. Don't give up. Writing for children is a very rewarding experience on many levels. If you truly love writing, any obstacles can be overcome with determination, persistence, and patience. You can succeed and you can reach your goals. But you have to want it.

Granted, there are thousands of writers out there on the same path as you. But what you may not realize is that only a small percentage of these writers conduct the proper research to find a publisher that fits their book. Only a few do the needed market research. Only a few write and rewrite constantly until they get it just right. Only a few follow the individual submission guidelines of the publishers.

Even if you do receive a rejection letter, don't lose heart. That doesn't necessarily mean that your manuscript is not publishable; it may simply mean that it wasn't right for that particular publisher. We will deal more with rejection letters in Chapter 13, but for right now, just know that a rejection letter is not the end of the world, nor should it be the end of your writing.

Thousands of children's books are published each year, which means that thousands of writers are needed each year. If you play by the rules and learn all you can about children's publishing, you stand a chance at success. Children's publishing is a very competitive and challenging field, and even the most talented authors can't always succeed on their talent alone. That's why it is so important to arm yourself with as much knowledge as you can and use that knowledge to give you an edge.

# Be Open to Criticism!

There are several venues open to writers to help them strengthen their skills, have their questions answered, and learn more about the craft. Whether you are a beginning writer or a seasoned author, you will benefit from taking advantage of one or several of the options explored in this book.

Before you sign up for any organized activity for writers, you need to first understand (and accept) that your work is going to be criticized. This isn't to say that people are going to shout out how awful it is, but it does mean that people will assess your work and you will most likely find out that it isn't perfect.

## Helpful Hints

Remember that when someone is criticizing your work, that is just it—they are criticizing your work, not you personally. Also try to remember that they are not criticizing to put you down, they are trying to help you make your work better, something you should be open to as a writer.

Learning to accept criticism is not an easy thing to do. Your work is a part of you, and it is easy to regard criticism as a personal insult. But sometimes that close relationship with your work will hinder you from looking at it objectively. That's where criticism steps in. Once you finally decide to release your work from the shelter of your safe-keeping, it is open to interpretation. Getting the objective opinion of several people before sending your work off to a publishing company will help to make your work the best it can be as well as prepare you for the criticism that you will most likely face from an editor.

### Go Outside Your Family

While it is always good for the ego to get the opinion of family and friends, their opinions are probably going to be biased. They might exclaim that it is the best story they have ever read or shower you with other such niceties. This of course is always pleasant to hear, but it really isn't going to help you better your work. If you truly want constructive criticism, show your work to people who don't know you, or at least not very well. They will be more likely to give you an honest opinion. Writer's groups, classes, and workshops are good places to get and learn from criticism.

If you decide to join a writer's group or take a writing class, criticism will definitely be on the agenda. In these forums, people work together to help one another better their work through the use of criticism. You will either read your work aloud or pass out copies for people to read on their own. You can expect to hear or read suggestions for improvement or questions about the story. This will almost always be conducted in a constructive manner so you needn't feel as though you are being attacked. These people are there first to help themselves and second to help you. Keep that in mind and open yourself to their ideas.

## Groups and Organizations

You will soon learn whose opinions are well thought out and supported and whose are watered down and vague. Use your best judgment. You needn't feel as though you should make every change that others suggest. The goal is to get your work as close to perfect as you can. With this goal in mind, you will find criticism to be quite helpful and may even come to welcome it.

Of course, the story is always your own and you have the final authority. You can either take or leave the suggestions of others. But if you truly want to make your work the best it can be, you will at least consider everything that has been said of your work.

A writer's group is an excellent forum for feedback and sharing information. Here you will meet other writers who are facing the same challenges you are. It is always comforting to know that you aren't the only one out there struggling to make your dreams come true.

Several communities have writer's groups already established. In your local area, check with libraries, schools, and community bulletin boards for any information about writer's groups. There are even some groups on the Internet, where you can post your work and many members can critique it electronically. If you come up empty-handed on finding a writer's group, start one yourself!

## Helpful Hints

Starting your own writer's group is a great way to make contacts and get feedback on your own work, not to mention reading other writers' stuff! Advertise at local libraries and bookstores, and don't forget that word of mouth travels faster than anything.

Writer's groups don't have one set agenda. Some gather solely to critique one another's works. Some are open to anything concerning the publishing industry such as discussions about market trends, contracts, editors, and reviews. Some will bring in guest speakers from time to time such as a published author or editor. Some simply combine all these elements and go with the flow. Whatever type of group you choose to join (or start), you will find it a rather casual and comfortable atmosphere in which to further your knowledge of the writing process.

### Benefits of Groups

Take advantage of the shared information. Since everyone will have a different background and know different people, the scope of information available will have a wide range. Perhaps one member is a former editor and can give you insider information on the publishing industry. Another may be the mother of ten children who can give you advice on how to make your child characters realistic. You may be able to score invaluable contacts through one or several of the members.

As an aspiring author, you will benefit tremendously by joining a writer's group. Not only will you learn from shared information, but you will also find the support that you might not otherwise receive. Working in a busy office, you constantly have the support of your colleagues, even if the support is only in the form of their physical presence. Writing, on the other hand, often leaves you with the feeling of isolation and lack of support. Since writing can be a very lonely occupation, it helps to get out of the house and meet with others who are traveling a similar path.

You will probably become good friends with other members of the group. While it is always good to have friends, this may actually put a dent in the usefulness of the group. Oftentimes, friends are hesitant to say anything negative to you. During a critique of your work, you may find that your newfound friends only praise you. Of course, it is nice to hear, but it defeats the purpose of the group. On the other hand, a minor disagreement between friends can trigger an unnecessarily harsh critique that may crush the dreams of the aspiring author.

If you feel that a friendship is affecting the usefulness of the group, say something. Let it be known that you are open to and welcome constructive criticism. If there is a tiff affecting the critique, try to get it solved or at least reach an agreement that it will not carry over into the group.

### Consider Taking a Class

Perhaps you have fantastic ideas for children's books, but when you sit down to actually write them, you find that your writing skills aren't quite so fantastic. Don't take this as an omen to give up writing. Instead, congratulate yourself for recognizing a weakness and do something about it!

## Helpful Hints

Taking a class at a nearby learning institution is a good place to start. Visit local colleges and universities and pick up a copy of their course listings (you may want to check out the adult education or continuing education departments for these). Browse through and highlight those classes that would help you to strengthen your skills.

Before you rush to sign up for a full course load, consider the time you have available to devote to a class. You will find day and time schedules next to the course listing. Check your own schedule against them and make sure that you can allocate the time. (You must also take into consideration the time it will take to commute to and from the school.)

Don't forget that you will probably be paying for these classes as well. Although a class description may look interesting, is it really something that you need? Keep in mind that to get your money's worth, you have got to learn. This means attending every class you possibly can, devoting your attention to the instructor during class time, and of course doing your homework. Taking a class is a big responsibility. Make sure you can dedicate the time and energy before signing up.

### Correspondence Courses—For the Writer on the Go

While local schools will most likely offer the courses you need to strengthen your language skills, not all of these will offer courses specifically on children's writing. If you already have a good foundation of language skills and want to take a class that teaches you to take these skills and use them to write for children, then you may need to explore outside your local area.

Often, distance learning courses for children's writing will advertise an instructor who is a published author or editor. While this is very appealing, you should check the credentials of the instructor before jumping on board.

If you are having difficulty finding a suitable course, it may help to post an inquiry on a children's writing message board or in a chat room devoted to children's writing. Other writers may be able to tell you what has and hasn't worked for them. If you are a member of a writer's group, ask the other members. Word of mouth is a great way to locate a reputable correspondence and online course.

## Helpful Hints

There are several correspondence and online courses available that may meet your needs. If you conduct a search on the Internet, you will undoubtedly hit upon several sites. You need to be picky about your choice. Don't sign up for the first class you find. Browse through several Web sites and request more information for those that you think would best suit your needs, including tuition, additional fees, and the class curriculum.

### Seminars and Workshops

Several writers find that participating in workshops and seminars is a great learning experience. The advantage of seminars and workshops over writer's groups is that you will most likely meet different people each time you attend. Therefore, you will be getting more critiques, more information, and more contacts. However, while writer's groups are often free get-togethers, you will almost always pay a fee for attending a seminar or workshop. If you can afford it, attend all the seminars and workshops you can; you will be pleased with the amount of knowledge you gain. If money is a little tight, go as far as you can with free critiques and information sharing before thinking of paying the sometimes hefty sums to rub elbows with strangers.

### Getting Your Money's Worth from Seminars

Seminars are often conducted in a manner similar to classes. Normally the main attraction is the speaker. Seminars featuring bestselling authors and top editors are often advertised nationwide. Therefore, if you attend one of these seminars, chances are you will have the opportunity to meet and make friends from all over the country. It always helps to have friends in the industry; you never know when a contact made through a friend will turn out to be the key to your dreams. The more widespread your friends, the more widespread your contacts. Just something to keep in mind.

There are also more localized seminars that still feature experienced authors or editors, but perhaps not as well known. These are no less educational than the others, so don't snub them. Plus, you probably won't have to pay as great a sum for these as you would for the nationally advertised seminars.

Seminars are often advertised in trade publications and through writer's organizations, as well as on the Internet. If you are interested in attending a seminar, be prepared to pay a fee. Make sure the seminar covers a topic of interest to you and check out the agenda before signing up.

### Workshops Can Work for You

Workshops are scheduled for one specific period of time, whether that is an afternoon or a week. Sometimes workshops are even tied into a vacation activity, such as skiing, or they can take place at fancy spa resorts. Depending on the hype that surrounds a workshop, you will sometimes be gathering with people from all over the country. Of course, there are also more regionalized workshops with fewer frills and less advertising that serve the same purpose.

The activities are often very similar to those of writer's groups. While the agenda varies, you will almost always have an opportunity to "workshop" your work. This can take place with either a large or small group of people. Sometimes you will have an opportunity to work one-on-one with a professional in the industry.

If you are interested in attending a writer's workshop, look through trade publications, search the Internet, and ask around. But make sure you know what you are getting into. Who will be conducting the workshop—is it an experienced author or editor? How much does the workshop cost? What is included in the cost? What is on the agenda? How much personal attention will you receive? While you will certainly gain some knowledge from any workshop, try to get the most for your money.

# Chapter 4

# Research and Cultivation

There's no getting around it: You need to arm yourself with knowledge of the marketplace. It is important for a writer to be aware of what is happening in the world of children's publishing, not only to maintain an edge that many other writers don't have but also to discover the best way of reaching the intended audience.

## Knowledge Is Power

Knowledge is power. Ignorance is bliss. As a writer, you want the power. It is unlikely that you would give a speech on cold fusion in front of thousands of people if you had no knowledge of the subject. Nor would you walk into an interview without the slightest idea of what the company does. Well, neither should you try to convince a publisher that your manuscript should be turned into a book without the knowledge of what is currently selling. The more knowledge you have of the market, the better chance you stand of getting the attention of an editor.

You must keep in mind that publishing is a business, and the success of publishing companies relies on their ability to sell books. If you think that publishing exists only to bring great literature to the world, you are living in an alternate reality. As a writer aspiring to get published, you can't ignore the business aspect.

Unfortunately, most editors will first look at the marketability of a book and then look at its quality. If you want your manuscript to make a good first impression, your best bet is to show your knowledge of the marketplace and how your book will thrive within it. You will not be able to write a convincing query or cover letter without the power of knowledge backing you.

### What to Watch for in the Market

There are several things you will need to keep an eye out for. Pay attention to what is selling well. Read reviews of new children's books and interviews with both up-and-coming and seasoned authors. Find out what books children and their parents are asking for at bookstores and libraries. What subject matters are being tackled? What topics have been beaten to death? What subjects are popular in the different age ranges? Are there differences in what girls and boys read? Are hardcover books or paperback books more prominent? What are popular trim sizes and page counts? The questions are endless, but you get the idea.

### Helpful Hints

Watch the news, listen to the radio, and read magazines. Train yourself to give attention to anything at all that may affect children's books and the publishing industry. There are several adult topics and issues that trickle down into books for children, such as AIDS or terrorism. These are issues that affect children as well!

Aside from the books themselves, keep track of the publishing companies. Mergers and acquisitions happen all the time, and you will need to know who is who and who is not there anymore. You will also have to know what type of books each publishing company produces. Some publishing companies produce only children's books, some produce only adult books, and some produce both adult and children's books. And within these broad divisions are subdivisions depending on what subject matter and type of books are published. There is a lot to learn and a lot to keep up with, but you will find the time and energy well spent when you see your book sitting alongside other great children's books on the shelf.

## Understand the Big Picture and Stay Up-to-Date

Before you begin researching the specifics of the children's publishing industry, you should take a look at the big picture. By understanding the various markets available to children's books, you will then be able to make choices concerning your own writing and take steps to zero in on specific areas. Keep in mind that the following markets are quite broad and allow room for a wide variety of subject matters and styles.

### Mass Market

Mass market books are paperbacks that are lower-priced, lower-quality books sold in supermarkets, discount department stores, newsstands, drugstores, and so on. Mass market books normally have a smaller trim size and are designed to appeal to a different audience from the one that buys trade books.

Mass market children's books are often tied in to a popular show or character. The publishers often come up with the concept and then search out authors to follow their guidelines. While it is not likely you will pierce the mass market with your own story ideas, it is possible to be hired as a writer for a preconceived line of mass market titles.

### Trade Market

Trade books are most often defined as books that are sold in bookstores. These books are usually higher-priced, higher-quality books that can be either fiction or nonfiction. While most think of trade books as hardcover books, trade publishers also produce paperbacks. The trade market is what most people think of when they think of bookselling. Unless you have a very specific idea of what you want to write, most likely you will be writing for the trade market.

### Institutional Market

The institutional market covers both schools and libraries. Someone has to write and publish the textbooks kids use in schools, right? Often textbooks are curriculum-based and developed by the publisher. However, not all books in the institutional market are nonfiction textbooks; schools are beginning to add more and more single-title books to their curriculum. Therefore, you can find publishers who produce high-quality fiction and nonfiction books that can be sold to bookstores, libraries, and schools.

Titles in the institutional market span a wide range of subjects. While there is certainly a need for those books in basic subjects such as science, health, and math, there is also a need for books covering topics such as death, aging, suicide, divorce, disability, and special needs.

### E-market

The electronic market is comprised of CD-ROMs, e-books, and other such multimedia products. Because children are certainly becoming proficient in the use of electronic and multimedia devices at young ages, publishers thought they had big business in meeting their needs and wants. However, the electronic market hasn't taken off as predicted.

That doesn't mean it won't; publishers have just decided to take a step back and slow down a bit. As for now, the electronic market is mainly comprised of nonfiction reference titles. But keep your eye on it. New technological advancements are made every day and the publishing industry isn't immune to their appeal.

**Where to Begin**

An easy and pleasurable way to begin your research is to visit a bookstore or library. Give yourself ample time to peruse the shelves. Pick up those books that catch your interest and look them over carefully. What made you pick up the book? Was it the subject matter, the cover design, the title, the author? Perhaps you have read reviews or heard the book mentioned through word of mouth. Is it a book you would want to read to your own children?

## Helpful Hints

If your finances permit, don't hesitate to buy at a bookstore or borrow from a library some books that caught your eye. Reading on your own can spark inspiration!

If you have a local children's bookstore, this is a perfect location to conduct initial research. If you aren't able to visit a children's bookstore, then take a stroll through the children's department of any bookstore in your area. What do you notice first as you walk in?

Pay attention to the books set up with displays as well as those books that sit on the shelves face out as opposed to spine out. Note the publishers of these books. If at all possible visit a particular bookstore on a regular basis and record how long certain books are on display.

Talk to a clerk and explain that you are an author researching children's books. He or she will be able to tell you what books are in demand. Find out what books children are asking for as well as what books adults are asking for. You may also inquire whether there are any topics not currently covered in children's books that customers are on the lookout for. If you are able to visit a children's bookstore, you will probably find that the clerk can offer all kinds of valuable information.

Libraries also offer a wealth of information for the eager researcher. In bookstores, adults normally make the purchases; in libraries, children normally check out their own books. You may find that the popular children's books in bookstores aren't the same as those in libraries. Note the differences.

Again, look for displays and note how long the library features particular books. Are there any books face out on the shelves? What books are lying on the tables or scattered in play areas?

Observe the children there. What books do they pick up and what are their reactions to those books? Do they seem to be searching for a particular author or are they just browsing? Take your own children to the library. Where do they go first? Once they have chosen their books to check out, see if they can tell you why they chose those in particular.

Talk to the librarian. Sometimes libraries have waiting lists for popular books. Find out what books are on these lists. If the library organizes regular activities such as story time, find out what books are featured and which are the most popular with the children. Sometimes libraries coordinate summer reading programs in which children check out and list the books they read. You may be able to get copies of some of these lists.

### Helpful Publications

There are quite a few publications you can peruse that will help you stay abreast of the constant changes taking place in the world of children's publishing. The following sections highlight some of these publications; but there are a number out there, so don't limit yourself to only those noted.

#### Trade Magazines

*Booklist* (*www.ala.org/booklist*) is a monthly magazine containing
    book reviews, and is published for librarians.

*Publishers Weekly* (*www.publishersweekly.com*) is a magazine
    devoted to the publishing industry; it offers current
    market information and publishes a new children's books
    announcement issue twice a year.

*Horn Book* (*www.hbook.com*) is a bimonthly magazine that contains reviews of children's books and feature articles on issues pertaining solely to children's literature.

*School Library Journal* (*www.slj.com*) is a monthly magazine that contains book reviews, and is published for librarians.

## Newsletters

*Children's Book Insider* (*www.write4kids.com*) is a monthly newsletter for children's writers offering writing tips, market information, submission tips, advice from authors, and articles covering a variety of topics in the children's publishing industry.

*Children's Writer* (*www.childrenswriter.com*), published by the Institute of Children's Literature, is a monthly newsletter for children's writers offering market information and articles on the writing craft, publishers, and editors.

## Writer's Magazines

*Writer's Digest* (*www.writersdigest.com*) is a magazine for writers and offers articles on agents, contracts, self-publishing; interviews with professionals in the industry; and occasionally news on children's publishing.

*The Writer* (*www.writermag.com*) is a monthly magazine offering submission tips, market information, and informative articles for all fields of writing.

## Children's Magazines

While magazines designed specifically for children will not provide information on the publishing industry's ins and outs, they do provide an insight into children's interests, such as *Highlights, Cricket,* or *Jack and Jill*. If you subscribe to a variety of magazines, you will be able to compare repeated topics and how they are handled. There may also be advertisements for or reviews of current children's books.

If there is a section contributed by the readers, pay particular attention to it. For instance, maybe the magazine allows children to write letters to the editor or showcase their own stories and artwork. Here you will find what is in the heart and souls of these children.

## Fall into the Market Gap

Finding a gap in the market is an author's dream. During your research you may come across topics that are currently unexplored in children's publishing, but desirable to children. If this happens, jump on it. Tapping into unexplored territory can be both exciting and lucrative.

Although it may seem as though every subject has been covered already, we are creating history every day. New technologies emerge, new discoveries are made, new events take place, and new issues are brought to the forefront. If you specialize in a particular area, whether it be science or woodworking, you are already aware of the latest happenings in that area. Could any of these advancements be turned into a children's book?

Finding a gap in the market doesn't necessarily mean that the subject has to be brand-spanking-new. You may find that an existing subject has not yet been explored in the form of a children's book. Or maybe it already has, but the book may be out of print or outdated. Can you give a fresh take on an old book?

If you believe you have discovered a subject that has not already been explored and would make a fantastic children's book, don't rush to contact an editor shouting that you have his or her next bestseller. Just because your research hasn't come across a book on that particular topic doesn't mean that it doesn't exist. Dig further into the depths of your research and make sure that you can't locate a book at all similar to yours. You certainly don't want to contact an editor and heighten the editor's expectations only to hear his or her voice— tinged with disappointment and annoyance—telling you that the subject matter has already been tackled and bombed in the children's book industry. Do your homework and be prepared.

### Direct Your Attention

While it is best to stay up-to-date on all aspects of children's publishing, if you have already decided what type of book you would like to write (or have already written) then you will also want to zero in on that during your research. For instance, if you are a history buff and interested in historical fiction picture books, then you should search the market for books of that kind and see what their track records are.

### By Topic

Take a close look at all the books covering your topic and compare them to yours. How is your book different? What does it offer that the others don't? You will have to convince an editor that yours has an advantage that the others don't; therefore you must know the market for these books. You also need to find out how well these books sell.

## Helpful Hints

Be ready to demonstrate to an editor that your book is special and has the advantage over similar books. At the same time, be reasonable if you are denied publication because of the market, something the editor has no control over.

Research the media and look for updated information or statistics concerning your topic. If you can improve upon or add a new twist to a topic that has already been covered extensively, then you might have a shot at grabbing an editor's attention. On the flip side, if the topic has had little play, then you need to consider why. Is the topic too boring for children? Perhaps other writers simply haven't been able to make it exciting. Or it may just be that the topic does not make for a good children's book.

### By Type of Book

Perhaps you don't know exactly what topic you want to cover, but you may know what type of book you want to write. For instance, maybe you are fascinated with picture books and can't see yourself writing anything but. Or maybe you want to deal only with the facts and prefer writing nonfiction. Whatever your fancy, you will still have to research the market.

Let's say you want to write chapter books. See if bookstores and libraries have a particular section devoted to chapter books. If so, you are in luck. Take an afternoon and don't stray from that section. Pick up every book that catches your eye and flip through it. What topics do chapter books explore? How many pages do they have? How are the covers designed? What are the trim sizes? What sets these books apart from the rest of the types of children's books?

Try to find out what chapter books are the most popular with children—and with adults. Compare the chapter-book section with the picture book, early reader, and middle-grade books. Which section is the largest? Which is the smallest? Ask around to find out what chapter books are the best known to kids and adults, not just booksellers and librarians. Also try to find out what books were disappointing to readers. If you can determine what helps a book to sell and what causes it to fail, you will have a head start on writing a successful chapter book.

Of course, you will also want to pay attention to new releases and interviews with chapter-book authors. Read through industry publications and find out what's happening in the world of chapter books. Which publishing companies publish chapter books? Keep an eye on these and how they market their product.

## Notebook, Your New Best Buddy

Before you can begin to write, you must have an idea. This is the starting point for all writers and must be handled with care. This section shows you how to organize the ideas you already have, how to capture new ideas, and how to focus on one idea so you can begin writing.

Maybe your mind is swarming with ideas, or maybe you are constantly on the lookout for that one great idea that will produce a bestseller. Whatever may be the case, you must get these ideas down on paper eventually, so why not start now and get a jump start on the process?

It's happened to all of us: You are hit unexpectedly by the best idea you've ever had, but when it comes time to make use of that idea, it is forever lost in the crevices of your mind. This can be very disappointing and discouraging even, but you can easily keep this from happening. Invest in a small notebook to carry around with you at all times. You never know when a great idea will strike you; but if you are prepared, you can jot it down right then and not have to worry about trying to remember it.

Jot down everything that catches your interest. Don't worry about trying to piece together an entire story from one observation. Just write it down and move on to the next thing that pops into your head or catches your eye. If you spend time concentrating on one idea, you are going to miss out on other observations and ideas that may be quite useful in a children's book.

There isn't a right and wrong way to write down your ideas. You can use abbreviations, pictures, full phrases, quotes, or fragments. Feel free to write outside the lines, diagonally, or even backward if that's what works for you. It's important that you capture as much of the idea as possible. Don't waste time writing neatly between the lines and in a grammatically correct way. These are just ideas, not a manuscript for submission.

Because you are ultimately going to organize these ideas later, it is a good idea to separate your ideas by story. For instance, you may come up with an awesome title, but that's it, you don't have any other ideas for that story. Write that title on one page of your notebook and leave the rest of the page blank. Don't write an idea for a different story on that same page or you might try to put the two together later on and become confused. If you later come up with character descriptions that will go along with your awesome title, flip back to that page and put the character descriptions there. If you can organize as you go, you will find it much easier to get everything in order later when it comes time to actually write a story.

## Helpful Hints

When your mind is swimming in a sea of ideas, you will want to write everything down as quickly as you can so you don't forget a thing. However, this could mean you could look at your notebook a few hours later, and see unreadable scribbles with lots of exclamation points. Try to use a system that organizes your ideas as you jot them down on your inspirational cloud.

You may find that you fill up notebooks quickly. In which case, you should either start buying in bulk or start thinking about actually writing. It is easy to put off writing by using the excuse that you are still gathering ideas. But if you have several notebooks full already, chances are you have a great story in there waiting to be written. Stop gathering and start organizing.

If you aren't one of those people who have a million ideas at all times racing around in their minds, you may be staring at a blank notebook wondering where to begin. Don't worry, the next few sections explore different ways to rouse ideas and help you start filling up those notebooks.

## Use Your Own Experience!

Write what you know. How many times have you heard that? Well, there must be something to it or it wouldn't be such a popular recommendation. Recalling your own childhood is a great way to start gathering ideas.

In Chapter 1, you were asked to create a timeline of significant events from your childhood. If you aren't sure where to start, use this to begin your journey. While significant events can certainly inspire plots, try to remember the insignificant things as well. One small detail has the power to shape an entire story.

**Use the Street Where You Lived!**

Ideas for settings will be easy to come across if you consider your own childhood settings. Where did you grow up? Think about everything that surrounded you, from the items in your house to the geography of your location. Did you live in the country with forests or fields surrounding you? Did you live in the city and play games in the streets with neighborhood kids? Were you landlocked or did you live on the water? Maybe you had a special place you visited to be by yourself. Think about what made that place so special.

What was the weather like? Maybe you grew up in tornado country. Maybe you lived on a beach and know what it's like to prepare for a hurricane. Did you have traditional activities relating to the seasons? Maybe you didn't even have seasons.

Try to recall everything you can about the setting in which you grew up. Can you create an atmosphere for a story from the background you knew so well as a child? While the setting in which you live now would be quite fine to work with, you won't know it from a child's perspective—unless of course you currently live where you grew up. It is important to get a child's perspective to write believably for children. That's why it helps to recall things from your own childhood.

## Helpful Hints

Try to recall specific emotions you had as a child and what action triggered those emotions. For instance, perhaps you felt lonely when your big sister started school and you were left at home with no playmate. Maybe the death of a family member left you sad and confused. Can you remember the tingles of excitement as you tried to settle down for sleep on Christmas Eve?

Often children will build up an attachment to a particular item or habit. Maybe you had a blanket that you carried around with you constantly. Or perhaps you liked to twist your hair as a form of relaxation. How easy was it for you to give up your pacifier? Think about the things you had an emotional attachment to and what it took to break you of the habit (that is, if you were able to break the habit).

The imagination of a child is something to be treasured. Try to recall your own imagination. Did you invent a game for yourself and your siblings? Did you have an imaginary friend? Maybe you liked making up stories. Maybe you liked to pretend you were an astronaut. Make-believe is a child's way of exploring his or her creativity. Try to draw on your past encounters with make-believe to inspire creativity in your current stories.

Take a look around. The world is full of details just waiting to be picked up on and turned into a story. From major world events and issues to a phrase muttered by a child passing by on the street, there are millions of idea stimulants right in front of you. You just need to learn to open your eyes.

Walk down a familiar street and look for anything that is new or out of the ordinary. Maybe a tricycle was left in the driveway on its side. This may cause you to wonder why it wasn't put into the garage where it normally is. Was there an emergency at the house? Maybe the child was called in for lunch and isn't through riding the tricycle. Maybe the child is testing boundaries and seeing how far he can push his parents. Why was it left on its side? Maybe the child had exciting news to tell her parents and in her rush to get out of the seat, she knocked it over and didn't bother to pick it up. Maybe the child fell and, blaming the tricycle for the accident, got mad and kicked it until it fell over. See, the mind can take just one small detail and run with it.

### Be an Observer

Train yourself to look around as you walk along instead of just looking at the sidewalk and your feet. Pay attention to what kids are wearing, the looks they give one another, the looks they give adults, what a child says to his dog, or the color of a little girl's shoes. Whatever it is that catches your eye, consider it for a moment. Would you be able to make use of it? If so, jot it down in your notebook.

Have you ever sat on a train, noticed someone, and wondered what that person did for a living or if that person had any children or where that person was going? If so, you were beginning to create a story about that person. Try this with a child. Pick out a child from a public place (one you do not know) and look at him or her for a couple of seconds. Don't take any longer than that because you might raise the suspicions of a supervising adult; plus, you shouldn't need much time to get your mind in gear. Write down everything you make up about this child: name, hobbies, best friend, home life, age, favorite color, and so on. Don't concern yourself with storylines or plots just yet—unless that's what comes to mind. Right now you are just gathering ideas.

Pay attention and use your imagination. You'll be surprised at the number of ideas that you come up with just by looking around at seemingly ordinary things. And don't forget to bring your notebook along and write everything down!

### Use the Media!

If you are still searching for ideas, pay attention to the media. Newspapers, magazines, books, television programs, and radio offer all sorts of stories and happenings in the world. They might just spark an idea of your own.

While you may normally look to the media for entertainment or news, as a children's writer, you should try to train yourself to scan it for ideas. It might be distracting at first, but after a while it will just be second nature and won't take away from your personal enjoyment.

As you read the daily newspaper, keep an eye out for anything that could serve as a plot, character, or setting. For instance, you might read a small article about a local lifeguard saving the life of a young boy. You might then write a story about a young girl who gets herself into trouble by disobeying her parents and sneaking off to go swimming. You explore her range of emotions as she finds herself in danger, throughout the rescue, and once she is safe. Or you might decide to write a story from the viewpoint of the lifeguard. Or you might disregard the people in the article altogether and simply choose to use a beach as your setting. From just one small article, your imagination can take over and suddenly you have several possibilities to jot down in your idea notebook.

## Organize Yourself—and Research

Before you turn your ideas into stories, you should first get them organized. If you don't create an organizational system as you're gathering ideas, you may find yourself tackling a tower of paper when it comes time to use those ideas.

The same organizational system does not work for every person. Some people can't allow a single thing to be out of place before they begin work. Others have the messiest desk you've ever seen, but they know exactly where everything is. This section will give you some ideas, but you need to create an organizational system that you are comfortable with and that best suits your style.

First of all, you need some place to store the information and ideas you gather. A filing cabinet works best, but it isn't always reasonable to rush out and buy a six-drawer filing cabinet, especially if you are just beginning to gather materials. If you have the space to devote to a filing cabinet, keep your eyes open for good deals. Often, you can buy filing cabinets from companies going out of business or at secondhand office supply stores.

## Helpful Hints

Most office supply stores carry accordion-like file folders that allow storage of many papers in different compartments. These folders can be buttoned shut at the top and are very lightweight—ideal for carrying your ideas and notebook with you!

A drawer or box dedicated to your children's book materials will work, as will a large envelope. The aim is to keep all your materials in one place so they are easily located. For the time being, you may find that your notebook works just fine. But chances are, you will fill that notebook rather quickly and move on to the next. You need to organize those ideas so that they are easy to sift through.

To organize your ideas, you'll need to incorporate a filing system—whether it is for a filing cabinet, desk drawer, box, or a large envelope. If you can organize as you go, you will save yourself time. However, some people choose to organize their ideas only when they have a substantial amount to work with.

Find a way to divide your ideas and related materials into categories. You may decide to separate the character ideas from the plot ideas, or the newspaper and magazine clippings from the notebook ideas. You may want to divide your ideas into type of book (fiction, nonfiction, faction) or book format (picture book, early reader, chapter book, and so on). Do whatever works best for you, but be consistent.

It doesn't matter what type of organizational system you choose to use. The point is to make these materials easily accessible. If you leave loose papers lying around the house, chances are your ideas are going to be lost or turned into scrap paper for the kids to play with. Having worked so hard to gather ideas, you will want to take care of them. After all, one of them might just be a bestseller!

You can't spend all your time gathering ideas. At some point you will want to write a story. Of course, your idea collection should be the first place you look for inspiration. You certainly don't want all that time spent gathering to be a waste of precious writing time.

Before your idea collection becomes overwhelming, take the time to browse through it. Pick out one idea, read through your notes, and jot down anything else that comes to mind. Start a new file for this one idea—whether this file is a "rejected idea but with potential merit" file or a "new book" file is yet to be seen. This idea is going to be your main focus for a while, so make it a good one.

It may be difficult to pick just one idea. As you look through your collection, set aside those that are particularly appealing to you. When you go through this second pile, if not a single one stands out from the rest, you might just have to close your eyes and grab. Don't trouble yourself too much over this step. You'll eventually explore those other ideas later on so don't think of this as a final and all-important decision.

Read over your idea again, add anything that comes to mind, and then let it sit for a couple of days. Mull over the idea. What type of book is it going to be? Can you sketch out brief character descriptions? Can you follow the plot all the way through? If it is still an idea that you are excited about after thinking of it for a while, then you have the go-ahead to begin the research.

## Research

When you have the idea you want to work with, it's time to do a little research—a lot of research if the topic is nonfiction. Dig up materials on your topic at the library. Find out what other books have been written on the same topic and take a look at these. Sift through magazines, educational publications, newspapers, Internet Web sites, and even materials from private organizations. Check your sources and make sure they are reliable (especially if you choose to research on the Internet). You may even decide to conduct interviews with specialists in the field.

## Helpful Hints

Always, always, always give credit where credit is due. If research for your book came from another book, make sure to note it in your bibliography. It's just good ethics—and could save you from some trouble later on.

# Chapter 5

# Writing and Revision

ow it's time to get to the heart of the matter: writing your story. This chapter helps you get started on your story, shows you how to keep the writing process flowing smoothly, and offers tips and advice to help you get past those obstacles every writer faces. Are you ready to write?

## Getting Started

While it would certainly be nice to sit down and just let the story flow from your fingertips, most writers find that this rarely happens. Usually there is a lot of prep work to be done before the story begins. Don't be discouraged; the prep work can be a lot of fun and will make the actual writing advance smoothly.

First of all you need to make sure your workstation is set up properly. Do you have your "new book" file? Are your reference materials within reach? Do you have paper and pens? Are you comfortable? Try to eliminate all possibilities of distractions and interruptions. You need to focus on your work. You won't be able to concentrate if you have to get up and walk across the room for the dictionary constantly or if you are trying to eavesdrop on a television program that is on in the next room.

Read through your new-book file. Jot down any other ideas that pop into your head while you're reading. Don't ever assume that you will remember something. As you know, your idea won't incorporate all the needed elements for a children's book; therefore you will need to sketch out an outline so you are sure of where you're going and can remain on track while writing.

## Writing Nonfiction?

If you are writing a nonfiction book, you should have a well-defined topic. Be careful not to make the topic too broad. Narrow it down as much as possible and maintain your focus. You may want to write a one-sentence description of the book and put it up on the wall in front of you or on your computer—somewhere in your direct line of vision. If you ever feel yourself wavering from the main focus, read over your description again.

Before you begin writing, make sure you have all the sources you need within reach. If this involves several books, you may want to use sticky notes to mark specific passages or make notes. If you are especially industrious, you can use different colored sticky notes for your chapters. This will make referencing your sources quick and easy.

## Helpful Hints

As helpful as sticky notes and highlighted passages are, remember that if you overuse them, you no longer notice their importance. Think about it—if you cover your computer monitor with sticky notes or highlight every other line in a book, they don't stick out any longer, do they? Use moderation.

Your outline should be divided into chapters. Give each chapter a working title and list the points you want to cover in that chapter. Remember that this is just an outline. It will help you organize your thoughts and develop your line of progression throughout the book.

However, it doesn't mean that this outline is set in stone. As you conduct more thorough research, you may find that you need to alter the outline somewhat.

### Writing Fiction?

Fiction may be a little more difficult to sketch out; it's not quite as straightforward as nonfiction. Before you begin writing fiction you should answer the following questions:

- What will be the format of your book (picture book, early reader, chapter book, middle grade, or young adult)?
- Will you write in first person or third person?
- How will you begin your story?
- What happens in the middle of the story?
- How will you end your story?
- Will you write in past or present tense?
- Can you define the theme?
- Where does your story take place?

Again, try to come up with a one-sentence description and post it in view to help keep your focus. Answering the previous questions will certainly help you to begin writing, but there is one more thing you will need to know inside and out if you want to get your writing endeavor started off right: the characters.

## Characters and Dialogue

You need to know your characters intimately before beginning to write. It helps to think of your characters as real people instead of figments of your imagination. You should know what they look like, their likes and dislikes, any idiosyncrasies they may have, and personality traits. If you believe your characters are real people, it will be easier to write them as real people.

## The Main Character

The main character should be the most in-depth character. Because this character will be the most developed, you may want to start off with this one. Running through the rest of the character descriptions will seem much easier once you have the main character sketched out. Plus, the secondary characters may very well play off the main character in regard to their functions in the story.

## Helpful Hints

When writing your protagonist, try to make him or her a little older than the age range you are writing for. Children are fascinated by those slightly older than them.

Figure out as much as you possibly can about your main character before writing; don't expect it all to come to you as you go along. If your new-book file contained a character description, certainly start with this one. Create a character description by answering the following questions as well as any others you can think of that will help define your character:

- What is the character's name?
- What is the character's gender?
- What does the character look like (hair and eye color, height, weight, distinguishing features, and so on)?
- How old is the character?
- What are the character's pet peeves?
- What are the character's hobbies?
- What is the character's relationship to the secondary characters?
- What are the character's strengths?
- What are the character's weaknesses?
- Where is the character's setting (house, school, city, country)?
- Who are the character's friends?
- What is the character's family like?

Your main character is the one who will grow and develop throughout the book. Do you have a game plan for this growth progress? It isn't acceptable to simply have the character suddenly come up with the correct solution and end the story happily ever after. You will need to show how the character struggles with his or her progress, how he or she overcomes obstacles, and the thought process along the way.

### Secondary Characters

Your secondary characters don't need to be as detailed as your main character. However, they are still essential to the story, so you should know them as well before you start writing. You'll need to know the names, ages, relationships to the main character, and physical descriptions of these characters. Unless it relates to the story, you needn't go into such depth as personal strengths and weaknesses.

### Helpful Hints

For ease in reading, ensure that your secondary character's name does not begin with the same letter as your main character. Also, your secondary character does not have to be your main character's friend—try stretching your writing muscles and making him an enemy!

Because these characters won't be as well defined as the main character, it sometimes helps to give each one an individual quirk or habit that will help both you and your reader recognize and distinguish the character a little better. For instance, maybe your main character has a four-year-old sister who is constantly sucking her thumb. Or maybe the main character's best friend is superstitious and is always on the lookout for bad and good omens. Use your creativity to keep these characters from being only pawns in the story. Though they may not be as important as the main character, they still deserve their own identity.

You will also want to stay away from stereotypes. It is easy to give in to the temptation, but editors are looking for fresh and original characters. For instance, if you find yourself using that kind old lady doling out cookies and milk to the neighborhood kids, give her a flaw that will take away from her identity of perfection. No one is perfect and if you want to make your characters believable, you'll have to recognize that in your character descriptions.

### Developing Your Character's Voice

While your characters will most likely each have a different voice that will show itself through your writing, you need to establish your main character's voice before writing. This will put the finishing touches on knowing your main character inside and out.

A good way to find your character's voice is to create a mock journal in which your character writes daily. Because a journal is personal, your character will feel free to write what he or she feels without worrying about outside opinions. Create a week's worth of journal entries for your character. This should be sufficient to identify a style and voice that is all his or her own.

Keep this journal within reach while you write. It's easy to sometimes alter your character to fit the plot or a particular event. Remain consistent with all of your characters throughout. If you find yourself straying, read through the journal and character descriptions to get back on track.

### Dialogue

Using dialogue helps keep the text fresh and stimulating. For those learning to read, the use of dialogue also provides white space on the page without seeming to purposely give the reader a break. For these younger readers, white space is often a relief to see.

Writing dialogue is not as easy as it may seem. You want your dialogue to help move the story along and sound natural at the same time. It should have a purpose. You don't want to waste space in your story with common everyday speech that means nothing.

## Helpful Hints

Just as you shouldn't write dialogue that goes above your reader's heads, you also should avoid dialogue that talks down to them and demeans their intelligence. Use your dialogue to enhance your story.

One of the most difficult tasks a writer faces is making dialogue sound natural. The best way to achieve this is to listen to what people say and how they say it. How do children speak to each other versus how they speak to adults? Do the conversations among girls differ from those among boys? What about the conversations between boys and girls? Go to a playground or other common meeting place for children and record random conversations by either using an audio recorder or writing down the conversations verbatim.

### Realistic Speech Styles

Pay attention to the grammar and style. Do children always speak in complete sentences? Probably not, and if you consistently use complete sentences in your dialogue, it will probably sound unnatural. You may also find that people stammer, use the wrong word, pause while searching for what to say next, and repeat themselves over and over. While these are natural styles, they can also be very distracting. Would you really like to read the same sentence five times in a row? Use your best judgment and focus on the purpose of the dialogue. If a speech style helps to define your character or move the story along, then you can certainly use it. But keep in mind that hearing and reading are two different things. What you may be able to tune out when participating in conversation is something you will have to take notice of while reading.

Your characters will speak differently depending on their personalities. You may have a shy girl who hardly says a word at all and an outgoing boy who loudly expresses his opinion on everything. Try to match up speech patterns with personality traits. When you observed the conversations between children, surely you noticed that the children did not all speak alike. Make use of this in your story to help the reader better understand the individual characters.

You must be careful not to write your dialogue exactly as it is spoken. People are rather lazy with their speech sometimes and run their words together or leave off endings. For instance, you may hear the word "gonna" used frequently, but it is best to translate it into "going to" in your work. If you are writing for young readers, you don't want to lead them away from correct language while they are still learning. Even if you are writing for advanced readers who know better, it is still best to use correct language.

Lazy language will trip up readers and distract them from the purpose of the dialogue. Plus, oftentimes it just seems to become a jumbled mess. If a dialect or lazy language is required to develop your character or story, by all means use it, but don't let it carry over into the speech of other characters.

When writing dialogue, you also must be sure to identify the speakers. No one wants to retrace a conversation to figure out who is speaking. If you write straightforward conversation between only two people, it isn't necessary to tag each line. But if it goes on for a while, you will need to identify the characters every few lines just to keep things straight. Also be sure to start a new paragraph with each new speaker.

Using the word "said" is perfectly acceptable for a tag line. Don't feel as though you must substitute a variety of words for *said*. Using too many adverbs or an assortment of *said* synonyms will weigh down the dialogue. People are used to plain old *said* and can easily read through it without having to grasp any more than the identity of the speaker.

## Show, Don't Tell

If you take a writing class, the "show, don't tell" rule will almost always be brought up if not pounded into your head. This rule applies to all forms of writing—but children's writing especially. Because you are writing for children, you want to write action-packed stories. This doesn't necessarily mean you need burning buildings and extreme drama, it just means that you should always have something happening. A good way to keep the story moving is to show the action instead of simply stating that something happened.

It is easy for adults to succumb to the practice of telling when it comes to children. Children are told what to do all the time; the last thing they want is to be told what to think and feel when reading a story. As a writer, you must accept that children are exceptionally intelligent and are perfectly capable of figuring out things on their own. For instance, instead of simply stating, "Amy is shy," show Amy standing alone in a corner biting her nails glancing around but avoiding eye contact. Your readers will understand—maybe all too well—what the character is feeling.

Dialogue is useful when it comes to showing. Through dialogue the reader can gather what the character is feeling by what he or she says. But again, make sure the dialogue sounds natural. A child seldom simply states how he or she feels. For instance, how many times have you heard a child say, "I am angry with you"? Instead, the child may call you names, stomp off and tell you to leave him alone; or the child may say she wants to go home to her parents. Use dialogue to show emotion, thought, and feeling without turning it into a direct statement of such.

Another good rule of thumb is to choose the active voice over the passive voice whenever you can. This makes the text more stimulating and gives it an effect of movement. If you use the passive voice too often, the text seems lifeless and static. For example, compare the two following sentences. Which is more lively and better suited for a children's book?

The vase was shattered to pieces after it was thrown by Mary. Mary threw the vase and it shattered to pieces.

The first sentence uses a passive voice, which tells the reader what has happened. The second sentence uses an active voice, which shows the action. Can you tell the difference? If showing versus telling is still unclear, write a story using only the passive voice. Then write a story using an active voice. Read them both aloud and you should be able to hear a distinct difference between the two.

## Battling Writer's Block

As you well know, writing for children is no easy task. You can learn only so much from reading how-to books, and the rest you will have to learn on your own. If you are writing your very first book, you might be rather overwhelmed at the moment. It will get easier as you get into the habit of writing regularly and progress with several works. Don't feel as if you are alone out there. Writing for children isn't easy for anyone, even seasoned authors. Keep the following tips in mind; they will help you throughout the writing process:

**Concentrate.** Concentration is the key to writing well. You won't be able to focus on your work if you have several outside factors distracting you.

**Omit unnecessary words.** Children's books normally don't allow a lot of room for text, so you must make the very best of the space you have. Make every word count.

**Don't use clichés.** Your text should be fresh and original. Most editors consider the use of clichés to be lazy writing.

**Watch your tenses.** Don't start a story in present tense and finish in past tense.

**Create smooth transitions.** The lack of transitional phrases or sentences will make your text sound choppy and confusing.

**Take breaks.** If you schedule several hours of writing time, you need to take short breaks frequently. Stand, stretch, take a short walk, or anything else you can think of to take you away from the stresses of sitting in one position staring at a computer screen.

**Keep the number of characters to a minimum.** The fewer characters you have, the more room you have to go in-depth with each. A large number of characters will most likely confuse the reader.

**Don't go overboard with descriptions.** Use descriptions that are necessary to the storyline, and let the readers use their imaginations for the rest.

**Don't preach.** You can certainly convey an important message through your story, but don't tell your readers what to think.

**Begin your story with action.** You want to hook your readers with the very first line. If you spend time in the beginning describing the setting and giving the backgrounds of your characters, the readers will get bored, put the book down, and never pick it up again.

### When Your Brain Goes Blank

Nearly all writers suffer writer's block at some point during their lives—some even do so on a regular basis. Writer's block is simply that period of time when you stare blankly at your work without writing a single word. Your inspiration seems to have flown out the window and your brain has shut down. Writer's block can be very frustrating and will test your aptitude for writing. But you can't let it get the best of you. You are the one with the fantastic ideas and wonderful talent. Just as any job has obstacles, so does writing: Writer's block is an obstacle that you will need to overcome.

To overcome writer's block, you need to get to the root of the problem. Try to figure out what is causing you to stall. While there are several possibilities, quite often writer's block is caused by one of two things: fear or stress.

Whether you are just beginning or are a seasoned author, fear can get in the way of your writing. Perhaps you are afraid of this new venture and believe that you are not good enough to make it. Maybe you have been successful with a past book and are afraid your next is not going to meet the high standards set by your audience and publisher. If you draw on personal experiences for your writing, fear of exposure can affect you. There are lots of things you can be afraid of, but none that you should be afraid of. You are in control of your work and you have to keep that in mind. Search yourself and figure out if fear is holding you back.

Another common source of writer's block is stress. Perhaps you are working under a tight deadline. Maybe you have nine children screaming in the background while you are trying to work. Or you may have a loved one in the hospital whom you can't stop thinking about. Try to figure out if there are outside sources of stress affecting your ability to write. If you can't concentrate on your work, you will undoubtedly suffer writer's block.

Of course, fear and stress aren't the only factors that can affect your work, but they are good starting points if you are unsure of what is causing writer's block. Once you know what the root of the problem is, you can then take steps to overcome the problem. If you fail to recognize the heart of the matter, your current bout with writer's block won't be your last.

Unfortunately, there isn't one specific remedy for overcoming writer's block. While this book can certainly offer advice and strategies you might try, ultimately, you must figure out for yourself what works best.

One of the first things you'll probably want to try is just to write. Read over your notes, character descriptions, and single-sentence book description and write whatever comes into your head. Don't worry about grammar, spelling, and sentence structure right now. Your main goal is to get started. Once you have written something—even if it seems like nonsense—on paper or the computer screen, you may build up the momentum to overcome the writer's block standing in your way. This exercise works especially well if the root of your problem is fear.

If outside stresses are affecting your work, try to find a way to expel them even if for only fifteen minutes. For instance, if you are trying to work while your children are in the next room playing what sounds like a rambunctious game, chances are you won't get a lot done, if anything. Consider hiring a babysitter or pawning your children off on their grandparents for a little while. This will give you the peace you need to concentrate on your writing. Of course, all your outside sources of stress won't be taken care of simply by hiring a babysitter. But use your creative genius to find ways of putting those stresses on the back burner for the time you need to get motivated to continue writing.

## Helpful Hints

Sometimes the best way to conquer writer's block is to just get away and out of your workspace. Take a walk, play outside with your dog, do anything but think about your manuscript. Also, try reading an unrelated book. Sometimes reading someone else's written word can get your creative juices flowing!

If you are just simply stuck and can't think of any particular reason you are suffering writer's block, you may want to try some writing exercises that will loosen you up and take the pressure off writing a particular story. For instance, try a free-writing exercise in which you simply write whatever comes to mind. Don't concentrate on anything and don't stop to think, just write. Some people refer to this as stream of consciousness. It may help you to establish the momentum you need to begin or continue with your story.

You might also try a change of scenery. Maybe you have worked so many hours in a small corner of the house that you are beginning to feel suffocated and antsy without even realizing it. Grab a notebook and pencil and walk to the park or a coffee shop to write. A breath of fresh air may be just the cure for your bout with writer's block.

## Distance Yourself and Learn to Let Go!

Completing a book is a great feeling. Undoubtedly you worked very hard to take a fragment of an idea and turn it into a completed manuscript in which you were able to say all you wanted to say and express your thoughts and ideas appropriately. Hard work deserves a reward. So, before you do anything else with that manuscript, read through it and then take a step back. Now is the time to reward yourself. Take your time—a few days even. But in the midst of the celebration, let that last read-through mull around your brain for a while. Jot down any ideas you have for a revision.

You shouldn't have any contact with the tangible manuscript at this time. Let the partying die down and allow your excitement to subside somewhat before you go back to it. Even though you may be itching to submit your manuscript to a publisher, you need to first look it over with a critical eye. You want your manuscript to be as close to perfect as it can be before letting an editor see it.

To be able to critique yourself you will have to distance yourself from the manuscript. Pretend as though you are reading someone else's work. Try your best to clear your mind of your manuscript and look at it with a fresh eye. This will be rather difficult, but if you concentrate on separating yourself it will get easier as you progress.

You must read through your manuscript several times before it is ready for submission. During each stage you must concentrate on a different area of revision. If the idea of reading your book over and over is unappealing, perhaps you should stop where you are and seriously consider whether or not this extra work is worth it. If you, the author, don't want to reread your book, what are the chances that a parent or child will want to read your book several times?

During the first read-through, focus only on the content of the book. Do any questions pop into your head while reading? Are there any holes that need to be filled? Are you consistent with your characters? Has your main character grown and developed throughout the book? Does each scene tie in to the plot? Are you able to visualize the setting and each scene? Is your writing original and fresh or filled with clichés?

Consider creating a list of questions like these before reading through your manuscript. If you know what you are looking for before you begin reading, you have a better shot at catching content errors and noticing areas that need to be revised.

Once you're satisfied with the overall content, you need to read the manuscript one sentence at a time. Though you may wonder how you normally read if it isn't one sentence at a time, this is different. You will read one sentence, stop, and consider only that sentence.

Are there any words in that sentence that you could omit without losing its meaning? Because children's books have precious little space to work with, it is a good rule of thumb always to omit needless words. Can you improve on the sentence structure? Can you make the sentence more concise and clear? Does the sentence say exactly what you want it to say? Are you using an active or passive voice?

When you have answered all these questions (as well as any you come up with) for the individual sentence, consider that sentence's relationship to those surrounding it. Is it in the best place? Does it maintain the rhythm and flow of the text or is it jarring and different from the rest? Do you want it to stand out?

While it may seem daunting (and time-consuming!) to put so much consideration into one sentence at a time, know that this will not only benefit the finished product but help you write better in the future.

## Helpful Hints

Some writers get so caught up in the revision process that the end is never in sight. Sometimes the story goes through so many revisions that it does not even resemble the original idea. Yes, you want to make your story the best it can be, but you also have to know when to say when.

Once you have completed the first and second read-throughs and made the appropriate changes, read through your manuscript one more time focusing only on grammar, punctuation, and spelling. Keep a dictionary and a style manual close by.

Are paragraphs divided where they should be? Have you placed speakers' words in quotation marks? Do you have too many exclamation points? Are commas in the right place? The checklist for grammar, punctuation, and spelling is endless, but you know best in which areas you are a bit weak and what to look out for. For instance, if you have a tendency to confuse *its* with *it's* (which is a common mistake), take care to double-check these throughout the manuscript. You may want to keep a list of commonly misspelled words close by as well as a personal checklist of difficulties you may have.

### Perfectionism

If you are a perfectionist, letting go will be hard for you. You have a great idea that will finally classify your story as perfect. You make the change. You read back through the manuscript, bask in its perfection, then discover that the change you made requires other changes to the manuscript for reasons of consistency. Sighing, you make the other changes only to find that the story has taken a different path and doesn't read nearly as well as it did in the first place.

Never fear, the cycle can be broken. First, give yourself a deadline. Write it down in your planner, stick a note to your computer, write it in big red letters on the wall—do whatever it takes to make the deadline real. If you convince yourself that you absolutely must meet that deadline, your mind will start prioritizing for you. You will find that suddenly your use of grammar becomes more important than changing the hair color of a secondary character.

Next, meet your deadline. If you have to strap yourself to a chair in front of your computer for sixteen hours a day, do it. You must not, under any circumstances, go beyond your deadline. The perfectionist in you will ensure that your spelling, grammar, punctuation, and other essential elements are met to the best of your abilities before you reach that deadline. By doing this, you will gradually learn to let go of those things that are not essential to your story and resist the temptation to rewrite a hundred times.

### Stuck on a Phrase

You may discover during the revision process that your favorite phrase—the very phrase the entire book was written around—needs to be cut. This phrase was part of the book from the very beginning. It was the first thing you added to the idea file. You love the phrase—it's a work of genius; it rolls off your tongue to charm all those who hear it; it sums up everything you want to say in just a few simple well-chosen words.

The phrase haunted you day and night, trying to worm its way into a story. Finally, you were able to use it to create a story. However, as you read back through your work, you find that the story has taken on a life of its own without a single regard to the importance of this phrase. The phrase stands out and sounds awkward when read alongside the other text. Everyone who has read the story has commented on it. So what do you do?

You could delete the text surrounding the phrase, and rewrite that particular section, though if the phrase does not have its place within the story itself, this will be a waste of time. You could delete most of the story itself and try to rework it to fit in with the beloved phrase. Or you could do what you know is best, though it pains you, and cut the phrase from the story. Let it go and know that you have made a great sacrifice to the craft of writing.

## Helpful Hints

Don't be so attached to an idea or theme that you let your story suffer. If something is not fitting correctly or seems to drag the story down, cut it out.

## Revision Checklist

While each children's book is different, there are some general things you want to keep in mind while revising. Use the following list of questions to help you along with the process, but don't rely solely on this. Also make those revisions that are specific to your story.

1. Is the plot appropriate for the age level you are targeting?
2. Has your main character grown and developed throughout the story?
3. Is the manuscript's length appropriate for the age level you are targeting?
4. Have you spell-checked your work? (Remember that spell-check is very helpful, but not the end all, be all. For example, spell-check will not catch a sentence like, "Amy went to school to learn how to read and right.")
5. Are your characters consistent throughout?
6. Is your story constantly moving?
7. Have you used dialogue to move the story along or help describe characters?
8. Have you omitted needless words?
9. Have you verified all facts?
10. Does the opening hook the reader?
11. Is your grammar and punctuation correct?
12. Does the main character solve the problem?
13. Have you kept your descriptions in check and left some things up to the imagination of the reader?

14.  Have you used the active voice instead of the passive voice?
15.  Are you consistent with point of view?
16.  Are you consistent with tenses?
17.  Have you removed all dated material from the manuscript?
18.  Does the dialogue sound natural?
19.  Do your characters each have their own identity?
20.  Does the manuscript read smoothly?

## Remember, It's Your Story

Let's say you have sent in a manuscript. You get a call from the editor and she tells you she likes the book. Your heart skips a beat. But then she says that she can't buy the book until it has been revised. Are you willing to do the revisions? Thinking that you may have left in a typo or spelled a word incorrectly, you agree. You receive the manuscript back and find an eight-page editorial memo outlining the extensive revisions that need to be made before the company will purchase your book. So what do you do?

You have two options. One, you can do the extensive revisions and give your manuscript a solid chance of being published. Two, you can take your manuscript elsewhere and begin the submission process all over again. The choice is up to you; after all, the story is yours.

However, before you make your decision, you should consider a few things. The children's publishing industry is very competitive. If you pull your manuscript from this editor, she will undoubtedly have another one waiting to take its place. If you stay with this editor, there is no guarantee you will be published, but the editor obviously saw something she liked, so you have a good shot at it. Also, keep in mind that wherever you take your manuscript, revisions will most likely need to be made before it is published.

# Chapter 6

# Getting a Leg Up!

To give your manuscript a much better shot at success, you need to find a publisher that publishes your type of book. All too often, the reason for the rejection of a manuscript is not the quality of the book, but that the writer has sent it to the wrong publishing company. This chapter will help you begin your search for that perfect publisher.

## Finding a Publisher

While there are several publishing companies that publish children's books, not all of these will be a good match for your book. Some companies specialize in a particular type of book. Some publish all formats, but only in a specific subject matter. Some publish everything. It is your job to figure out which is which. Your goal is to find a publisher that will welcome your book to its list. The only way this will happen is if your book falls into the category of books it publishes.

Before you can begin your search for the perfect publisher of your book, you need to answer a few questions about your book. The answers to the following questions will help you to narrow down the list of possibilities (which at this point is all publishing companies!):

- Is your book fiction or nonfiction?
- What type of book have you written (picture book, chapter book, etc.)?
- To which market(s) will your book be sold (trade, mass market, etc.)?
- Under what subject would your book be categorized?

If you are having difficulty categorizing your book, refer to your research notes. You should have already researched similar titles. Take a look at where these books are sold and where they are shelved. This should give you a good idea of what categories your book fits into.

## Gathering Info and Asking Around

Once you have categorized your book, start seeking out potential publishers for it. You could visit a bookstore or library and jot down the names of publishing companies that published those books that fall within the same category as yours. You could thumb through trade journals and note any publishers you come across that may make a good match. You could talk to the people in your writer's group and see if they have any suggestions. You could do a search on the Internet for children's publishers of your type of book.

## Helpful Hints

If you have never published a book before, that limits your options. Check out Web sites of publishing companies and see what they put out. If they feature a lot of high-profile authors, you probably won't get signed with that company. But send your manuscript anyway, you might have some luck!

Creating a list of the possibilities doesn't mean that you can send your manuscript to each and every one. Mergers and acquisitions are always taking place. The publishing company you may have come across during your search at a library may no longer be in existence. Or maybe the publishing company still exists but it no longer publishes your type of book. You will need to conduct further research to narrow the list of possibilities to a list of potentials.

It helps to create a master list of possible publishing companies. The more organized you are, the easier it will be to put together a manuscript submission or query letter. If you are computer savvy, you may want to create a database or spreadsheet that will eventually hold all the necessary information you will need for the potential publishers. If you aren't sure how to set up a database or spreadsheet, don't trouble yourself learning now—a notebook or file folder will work just fine.

Once you have a list of possibilities, you need to begin gathering as much information about them as you can. This will take quite a bit of time but is well worth it. Try to get a copy of each publisher's current catalog. Find out if it is an imprint, a major publishing company, or a small publishing company. What markets does it target? Does the company specialize in children's books, or does it have only a children's division? How many titles does it publish a year? Also jot down notes or clip articles from trade publications that pertain to these companies.

You will want to pull together addresses, phone numbers, Web sites, and contact names for each of these companies. Often, a publishing company's Web site can be a great source of information, including titles on their current list, backlist titles, submission guidelines, and contact information.

The following sections highlight places you may look to help you get started in your research. Of course, these aren't the only resources out there. Take your time and gather as much information as you can.

### Children's Writer & Illustrator's Market

*The Children's Writer & Illustrator's Market* is a handy reference guide to have on hand when researching publishing companies. The book is updated annually and provides listings of both book and magazine publishers specific to children's literature, and a description of what they publish. The book provides contact names, e-mail addresses, Web sites, submission guidelines, and pay rates.

This book also includes other valuable information such as guidelines for writing query letters and cover letters, mission statements from publishers, and articles on high-interest subjects such as contract negotiation and networking. You can find information on contests, awards, conferences, workshops, and organizations, as well as get advice from professionals in the industry.

### Literary Market Place

*The Literary Market Place* (often referred to as the LMP) is an annual directory of American and Canadian publishers. Here you will be able to find almost anything you are searching for within the publishing industry. You will want to concentrate on its lists of publishing companies. The listings include the name, address, telephone number, a description of what types of books the company publishes (young adult, general trade, textbooks, etc.), categories of books published (fiction, nonfiction, poetry, etc.), and contact names.

*The Literary Market Place* is quite expensive and you may not want to spring for the cost just yet. Fortunately, most libraries carry a copy in their reference departments—just be prepared to do a lot of copying. If you are interested in the information found in this gigantic book, you may also consider visiting *www.literarymarketplace. com*. Here you will be able to access limited information, including information on small presses and names and addresses of some publishing companies.

If you can afford it, you may subscribe to Literary Market Place. com and have access to the entire database, which includes everything in the print version. The database is easy to search and will help you to narrow down exactly what you are looking for, saving you a lot of time in the long run.

## The Children's Book Council

The Children's Book Council is a nonprofit trade organization whose members include U.S. trade children's book publishers. While you can't become a member, you do have access to its list of members. The list includes the publishing company's name, address, phone number, type and format of the books it publishes, and general submission guidelines. You will also be provided with contact names, though you will need to double-check them. You can get this list in either hard copy or by visiting the Children's Book Council's Web site. If you view the list from the Internet, you will also see that there are links to those publishers that have their own Web sites.

Keep in mind that, although this list provides a great deal of information, it is not complete. It lists only those companies that are members of the Children's Book Council. You will want to continue your research through other sources.

For more information about the Children's Book Council, visit its Web site at *www.cbcbooks.org*; write to The Children's Book Council, 12 West 37th Street, 2nd Floor, New York, NY 10018; or call 212-966-1990.

## Ask Around

While publications are great for gathering facts, sometimes you want more than just the facts. This is where word of mouth comes in. Talk to anyone and everyone you know who may be able to help you in your search for the perfect publisher. This includes anyone who is directly involved in children's publishing (such as an editor or sales representative), book buyers for bookstores, children's librarians, other writers, or literary agents. Remember that any information you gather, no matter how trite it may seem, may be put to use later on.

Do you know anyone who currently works in the industry? Contact these people and bring along your list of potential publishers. See if they can offer any insider information.

For instance, perhaps a friend tells you that a certain editor from your list has a deep-rooted pet peeve regarding animals that take on human characteristics in stories. In which case, your story about Larry the Lizard who talks and drinks coffee might not go over so well with that particular editor. On the other hand, a fellow editor in that same company absolutely adores lizards and has her own lizard farm. Of course, your manuscript would be better received by the latter, but you wouldn't have known that without the insider information.

You may discover that a certain publishing company is looking to produce a new series, though this news has not been made public. If your manuscript has series potential, you may want to include that in your cover letter, giving you a bit of an edge over other writers.

You may simply find out that your manuscript will not fit in with a particular publisher as you thought it would. Or maybe a publisher is working on a manuscript that is very similar to yours and probably would not include two such similar titles on its list. On the flip side, you may find that a new publishing company is emerging that would embrace your type of book or an already established company that is not on your list of potential publishers is looking to expand its children's department and your book might just find a home there.

It also helps to talk to other writers. If you have joined a writer's group, take your list of potential publishers to the next meeting. You may find out that another aspiring writer has already submitted a manuscript to one of the companies on your list. Perhaps the manuscript was declined because the company has decided not to sign up any more New Age books because they did not work well within the company's list. In which case, you would not want to bother submitting your Tarot for Teens book to that publisher.

You may get an idea of true response times (not those stated by the company) for some of these publishers as well. Once you have sent in a manuscript, it can seem like a lifetime waiting for a response. If you have a better sense of the response time, you will rest easier.

Maybe you have a long list of potential publishers and simply can't decide who to contact first. A fellow writer may be able to tell you which publishers are the best to work with from personal experience. It does happen sometimes that a publishing company gains a reputation of being difficult to work with—whether contracts are almost impossible to negotiate, advance checks are not paid promptly, or inexperienced writers are taken advantage of. It helps to know which companies are going to give you the best experience.

## Guidelines from Publishers

Once you have a list of publishers, write to each one requesting a copy of its writer's guidelines. Because each publishing company is different, each will have its own set of guidelines. Often these guidelines will detail what the company is looking for. The guidelines will usually explain what type of books the company publishes and what topics are covered.

The guidelines should also tell you whether or not the company is currently accepting unsolicited manuscripts. Unsolicited manuscripts are those that are not asked for by an editor or publisher. Your manuscript will most likely be unsolicited material, unless of course an editor has contacted you directly requesting to see your work.

### Helpful Hints

If the guidelines state that the company does not accept unsolicited manuscripts, don't try to send it in anyway. This tells an editor either that you haven't bothered to check out the guidelines or, even worse, that you have read the guidelines but decided not to respect them. Even though your manuscript may be a perfect match for the company's line of books, you can't force yourself on an editor. It is likely that your manuscript will not even be looked at, so don't waste the time, energy, and expense.

If the company does accept unsolicited manuscripts, you need to present your work in a professional manner. One good way to do this is to show the editor you have done your homework and are confident that your manuscript is right for that particular publisher. If your manuscript matches the criteria in the guidelines, you have a better shot at getting an editor's attention.

As you are researching publishing companies, you may come across advertisements from companies promising to publish your book. Finally! Someone understands the hardships writers face in trying to reach the shelves and has taken steps to make it easy, right? Don't be fooled by these advertisements. There is no easy way to get your book published, distributed to the proper markets, and into the hands of children. If becoming successful within children's publishing was so easy, everyone would be full-time children's writers.

Have you ever heard the expression "too good to be true"? These advertisements are just that. Normally, the companies behind the ads are subsidy publishers, AKA vanity presses. Subsidy publishers are indeed publishers and can publish your book, but the catch is that you pay for it. You pay a fee (sometime an exorbitant sum) and the subsidy publisher will turn your manuscript into a set number of books and deliver it to your doorstep. If you reach a point where you are unable to find a publisher that is a good match for your book or your manuscript has been rejected by all potential publishers on your list, you may find subsidy publishing tempting.

You are confident that your manuscript is top-quality children's literature. You don't understand why editors did not recognize the masterpiece they held in their hands. You don't really need to make a down payment on your dream home, you could continue to rent for a while. You can use that money to hire a subsidy publisher and show up the rest of the children's publishing world. Sounds good, doesn't it?

Unfortunately, subsidy publishers won't get you very far in the publishing world. They do publish your book, but the rest is up to you. Most likely you will have to market your book. You will have to raise awareness. You will have to take time out of your busy schedule to convince booksellers that your book is worth stocking on their shelves. You essentially become a publisher.

If you find yourself at a dead end and leaning toward subsidy publishing, don't give up and don't give in. Put your manuscript through another revision process or two. Do further research into publishing companies. Try to find another angle from which to pitch your manuscript. Or you may find that you just need to set it aside and begin a new project. If editors aren't jumping on your manuscript, there is probably a good reason for it. Chalk it up to a lesson learned, start afresh, and make that down payment on your dream home.

## Self-Publishing

Some people resist the temptation of subsidy publishers, and instead turn to the idea of self-publishing. You know that your book is worth publishing, so why not do it yourself? This way you don't have to bother researching publishing companies, abiding by writer's guidelines, convincing editors of your manuscript's worth, and facing rejection. Plus you get to design your own cover, illustrate the book however you please, charge whatever you want, and reap all the profits. The only problem is, you have to work very hard and know what you're doing to make a profit.

As you will find out later in the book, a publishing company does a lot more than just accept/reject manuscripts and send them off to the printer. You will have to learn the business in full if you wish to be successful with self-publishing—and you thought researching publishing companies was a lot of work. Not to mention the fact that you need to have the capital to get started. You can't make money without spending money in self-publishing.

Self-publishing requires that you take on the roles of several people. You will have to be the writer, the editor, the publisher, the art director, the designer, the sales rep, the publicist, and the accountant. Your book will need to go through the same process as those in traditional publishing. If you try to take shortcuts, they will show up in the quality of the book. Therefore you will need to hire a copy-editor, proofreader, illustrator, and printer.

While you may take pride in making all the decisions for your book, there are a lot of decisions to be made. Will the book be hardcover or paperback? What will be the trim size? What will be the price? Will you have color or black-and-white illustrations? Who will do the illustrations? How will you market your book? How many books will you initially print? What type of paper will you use? You must also decide on printing and binding companies.

You will have to design not only front and back covers but also the interior. If you include illustrations you will have to learn about art reproduction. You will have to assign an ISBN. You will have to find a way to get your book into stores. You will probably want to hire a distributor, but even so, very few people are willing to take a chance on someone who has not been previously published.

While all this only scratches the surface of the work involved, you get the idea. Self-publishing requires a huge commitment on your part. And don't forget the risk involved. This is a big decision to make. Do tons of research until you know exactly what you are getting yourself into before making a final decision.

Self-publishing is a lot of hard work, but it can also be very rewarding. If you are willing to invest the time, energy, and money, you can become successful. Others have done it before you and will continue to do so after you. However, it is essential that you know the publishing business inside and out. You can't take shortcuts and you have to make sure that your book stands up to the professional standards of those in bookstores and libraries.

While it is recommended that you first try to get published through traditional publishing houses, if you are determined to self-publish your work, then there are several reference guides available to you, such as *The Self-Publishing Manual* by Dan Poynter. You may also considering hiring a consultant to give you advice and show you the ropes so you don't feel as though you are completely on your own.

## An Agent's Job

A literary agent works as a go-between for writers and publishers. This includes sending the manuscript to editors, negotiating contracts, and handling payments and royalty statements. Both aspiring and seasoned writers find the aid of an agent quite helpful. They do in fact take quite a load of responsibility from the writer and can get your manuscript into the hands of editors you may not otherwise have had the means to reach.

It is an agent's job to know the ins and outs of the publishing industry. Agents are up-to-date on current market information. They know what publishers are currently publishing. They know what publishers are looking for. They know who to contact and most likely already have established relationships with these contacts. Bottom line: It is an agent's job to represent you and sell your work.

There are some publishing companies that do not accept unsolicited manuscripts. On your own, you would not be able to get the attention of an editor working there. Agents normally can. Agented manuscripts are able to find their way into the hands of the editor who would best be able to give your manuscript the consideration it deserves.

## Helpful Hints

Advice varies from agent to agent. Sometimes you will find an agent who is willing to sit down with the manuscript and edit it him- or herself, but since time is money, such agents are few and far between.

Unsolicited manuscripts normally find their way to the slush pile, and an editorial assistant is given the task of wading through it. Keep in mind that a high number of those manuscripts in the slush pile will either be inappropriate for that particular publisher or just flat-out terrible. Having yours mixed in with all the others doesn't always bode well. For one, you are relying on the opinion of an editorial assistant for your manuscript even to reach the desk of an editor. Second, you could be waiting several months for your manuscript to go through the needed channels, all the while wondering if you should send your manuscript elsewhere or hold out this particular publisher.

Agents can get your manuscript in the door and on the desk of an editor quickly. Agents also know just the right buttons to push with editors. It is their job to sell your manuscript. Therefore, they know what phrases and statistics to use; they know what aspects of the manuscript should be addressed; and they know how to build excitement and enthusiasm. In short, they are experts in the art of the sales pitch.

In some cases, an agent will go above and beyond the call of duty. Whereas a publishing company may simply send you a rejection letter without explaining exactly why the manuscript was unsuitable, an agent may decline the manuscript as is, but recognize the promise in your abilities and work with you to create a publishable manuscript. Agents are always looking to build the careers of writers. After all, if an agent's writer builds a successful career, the agent will also build a successful career.

Some agents will recommend hiring a freelance editor and provide you with contact names. Others will briefly state in a letter what you need to work on or what they would like to see done to the manuscript. In some cases, you may even be recommended to a different agent and provided with his or her contact information (be sure to conduct a background check before you hire anyone to edit your manuscript!). You really can't know what to expect from an agent's response, but if he or she is willing to help, you'd best listen.

## The Tradeoff

Sounds pretty good, doesn't it? Write a brilliant manuscript, get an agent, and leave the dirty work to someone else. As we all know, everything comes with a price, and agents are no exception. This, after all, is business.

### Monies

The good news is the publisher will pay the agent. The bad news is that it is your money the agent is taking a cut from. Because agents handle the monies and royalty statements, the check cut for your manuscript is sent to your agent. The agent takes a commission, which is usually 15 percent, and then cuts a check to you for the remaining money.

## Helpful Hints

Sometimes agents also expect to be reimbursed for certain expenses, including such things as postage, express deliveries, photocopies, long-distance calls, and so on. Be sure to ask if there are any additional expenses that you will be required to incur. Also keep in mind that these expenses should not be charged to you without your permission; anything deducted from your check should have been approved by you beforehand.

You will almost always have to sign a contract with the agent. The contract should cover the agent's compensation, how long the contract would remain in effect, and exactly what the agent is responsible for.

### Control

While having an agent take on the responsibility of submission certainly makes things easier on you, you have to understand that by taking on an agent, you have to give up some amount of control over your manuscript. Many writers simply can't handle this. You have to be able to trust that the agent is going to do his or her job to the best of his or her abilities. It is the agent's job to sell your manuscript. If you don't want to allow the agent to do his or her job, then you'd best not hire an agent.

If you have specific publishing companies in mind that you believe would be a good fit for your book, you can certainly pass the names along to your agent. However, it is unlikely that you will have direct control over the submission process. While a good agent will consider your suggestions, especially if you can back them up with reasons your manuscript would fit the company's list, the agent doesn't have to act on them. An agent's priority is to sell your manuscript, and he or she may not even take into consideration your thoughts on a particular publisher. He or she may or may not address your list of publishers first. You have to trust your agent's knowledge of the industry.

Also keep in mind that responses from editors will go through your agent. You may not even see them at all. You will also have to hand over control of contract negotiations. While a good agent will do his or her best to get you a good deal, and you have final authority over whether or not to sign the contract, you are giving up control of the actual negotiation.

## Where to Look

So you want an agent, but you aren't sure where to find one. Just as you go about finding the perfect publisher, you have to conduct a lot of research to find the perfect agent. If your primary motive for finding an agent is to avoid all the research you would have to do in finding a publisher, you may want to rethink your decision to get an agent. That said, there are quite a few places you can search for an agent, some more reliable than others. Start with those listed here, but don't limit your search to only these.

### Association of Authors' Representatives

The Association of Authors' Representatives (AAR) is an excellent resource for those interested in finding legitimate literary agents. The AAR has a strict canon of ethics that agents must adhere to in order to be members. For instance, to qualify for membership, the agent must have been practicing for at least two years and can't charge the client up-front fees.

You can find the list of members, which includes names and addresses, by visiting *www.aar-online.org*. You will also find here AAR's membership qualifications and Canon of Ethics. If you do not have Internet access, write to: Association of Authors' Representatives, P.O. Box 237201, Ansonia Station, New York, NY 10003.

### Literary Market Place

*The Literary Market Place (LMP)* is one of the top resources for the publishing industry. However, the *LMP* also includes a section devoted to literary agents, including international agents. Here you will find names, addresses, and specialties included in the profiles, among other information.

If you would like to use the *LMP* as a resource, consider visiting your local library. Normally a copy can be found in the reference section. Otherwise, you may visit *www.literarymarketplace.com*, although the Web site requires that you subscribe to its service to receive complete access to the information found in the *LMP*.

### Writer's Digest Guide to Literary Agents

*The Writer's Digest Guide to Literary Agents* is a handy guide for the author determined to secure the representation of an agent. Here you will find the necessary contact information for more than 500 literary agencies. You will also find submission guidelines and individual needs specific to each of these agencies.

While the book will certainly help you locate an agent, you must always do your own research. Also provided in the book are sample query letters, market information, and tips for finding the ideal agent.

### Agent Research & Evaluation

Agent Research & Evaluation (AR&E) is a company that provides a number of services to help you locate an agent. This is a business and they charge fees (ranging from $25 to $240) for most of their services. They conduct the research on agents and provide you with a detailed report of the agent's deals. If you can justify the cost, this can be a very valuable source of information for your research needs.

AR&E also provides a free service through which you give the company an agent's name, and it will tell you whether there is a public record on that particular agent and/or if there are any negative reports about him or her. You can also find a list of agents, though only names are provided. Visit *www.agentresearch.com* or write to Agent Research & Evaluation, 334 East 30th Street, New York, NY 10014, for more information.

## Know Your Agent!

Let's jump ahead a bit and say that you have an agent interested in representing you. While you may be overjoyed and certain that all your dreams are about to come true, you need to settle yourself down and take a rational approach. Do not immediately sign a contract with the agency. You need to find out a few things first:

- Ask if the agent is a member of the Association of Authors' Representatives.
- Find out how long the agent has been practicing and how long he or she has dealt with children's books.
- Discuss the agent's compensation and ask about any additional fees that may be charged to your account.
- Find out how involved you will be in the submission process. Will the agent notify you of all submissions and offers?
- What children's books has the agent sold?
- Ask for a list of references.
- Find out what the agent has currently sold and who his or her clients are.
- To what publishing companies has the agent sold books?

You will undoubtedly come up with your own list of questions, but certainly find out the answers to these. (The AAR's Web site *www.aar-online.org* also provides a list of questions to ask an agent.) Be cautious and go with your gut instinct. And of course, read over the contract carefully. Feel free to ask the agent to clarify anything you don't understand. If the agent is vague or unwilling to answer your questions, don't bother signing. You would likely be making a big mistake, and even if the agent is legitimate, you shouldn't be left in the dark when it comes to your precious work.

## Submitting and the Final Decisions

First of all, you need to have a completed manuscript before you consider getting an agent. Especially if you have not been published already, an agent won't represent you based only on your ideas. Make sure your manuscript has gone through the needed revision process however many times it takes to get it as close to perfect as you can. You must be confident in your work if you want it to go any further than your own desk.

### The Query Letter

While certain agencies may have their own submission guidelines, most often agents ask to be sent only a query letter at first. The query letter is your introduction. You should keep it very short and to the point. Don't let your letter go beyond a page. Put your writing skills to the test here.

You should introduce yourself and state that you are interested in finding representation for your book. Mention any works you have previously published. (Agents are more likely to take on writers who have already proven their abilities and have their work out there.)

State what type of book you have written (middle-grade historical fiction, fiction picture book, young-adult novel, etc.) and give a brief description. Keep it brief! Don't delve into the complex characters or give a play-by-play account of the plot. Also be sure to enclose a self-addressed stamped envelope for a response.

Proofread your letter, make sure your contact information is clear, and send it off. You may choose to send query letters one at a time or to several agents at once. There aren't any rules pertaining to this, but keep in mind that for an unpublished author, the odds are against you in finding an agent. Therefore, it may be best to send query letters in batches of, say, ten to save time. Don't be discouraged if your first batch comes back without an invitation to send in your completed manuscript; just go to the next batch and keep your fingers crossed.

## Helpful Hints

If you haven't been published, don't apologize or make excuses, just say nothing. But if you have any credentials that will help sell the book, mention them.

### Manuscript Submission and Final Decision

If an agent asks to see your manuscript or a sample, send it right away. You've already captured the agent's interest; don't give him or her time to forget you. Agents deal with several query letters a day, and until you are sold, you aren't the agent's main priority. Also be sure to follow the agent's instructions—don't send in a completed manuscript if the agent wants to see only a chapter.

Read over your manuscript one more time before submitting it. Watch for typos and make sure you haven't left in any notes to yourself. The submission should look clean and professional. Of course, the agent will probably dirty this beautiful work of art with his or her own comments and suggestions, but that's just part of life.

While a request to see your work is certainly a good sign, it isn't always going to land you an agent. You will probably be declined several times at this stage before you are offered representation. Finding a good agent is sometimes even more difficult than finding a publisher for the first-time writer.

The final decision, of course, is yours to make. But before you invest great amounts of time and energy into the search for a literary agent, take some time with the decision-making process. You will have to do a lot of work either way—whether you decide to find an agent or submit to publishing companies yourself.

On one hand, an agent who has agreed to represent you is sure of his or her ability to sell your manuscript. The agent already knows who to contact and how to pitch your manuscript. The agent has experience and expertise that you don't. The agent will be a big help in taking you through your first publication. The agent will be able to open doors that you couldn't open on your own. The agent will make sure you get a good deal and work with you to publish even more. A lot can be said for having a good agent on your side.

On the other hand, you don't need an agent to get published. While there are certainly several publishers of adult literature that do not accept unsolicited or unagented material, the children's publishing industry generally is more accepting of unsolicited material. You will need to know the market and the various publishers anyway, so why not be your own agent?

Money is also a big thing to consider. Normally an agent will take 15 percent of what you make. This can add up to a lot. You could always do the work yourself and keep all the profits. Plus, it can be harder for an unpublished author to find an agent than it is to find a publisher. In which case, the time put into finding an agent could have been better spent finding a publisher.

You also have the option of contacting publishers and pitching your manuscript yourself, and getting an agent when you reach the contract stage. This will give you complete control over your manuscript and the submission process. Several children's book publishing companies accept unsolicited manuscripts, so it is certainly possible that you do not need an agent to sell your work. However, many authors find contract negotiation to be a little over their heads, especially if they are first-time writers.

# Chapter 7

# Can You/Should You Illustrate?

Many children's books rely on illustrations to help tell the story. But who draws those illustrations and how are they chosen to accompany a particular book? Whether you are a writer without the ability to draw a recognizable stick figure or a professional illustrator trying your hand at writing, this chapter will help you better understand the process of putting pictures to words.

## To Be or Not to Be

Several aspiring writers mistakenly assume they need to provide illustrations for their picture books. Having looked at the variety of amazing illustrations in children's books today, you probably find this notion very intimidating. If you are a writer and not an illustrator, there is no need to worry—most often, publishers take on the responsibility of finding an illustrator for their books. If you believe you have the ability to illustrate your own work, you may very well have the opportunity to do so, but you need to take a long hard look at your work before choosing to submit it.

If you want to submit illustrations for your book, think about your qualifications. Because writing and illustrating are looked upon as two separate talents, you need to be able to prove that you are adept at both. Do you have a degree from an art school? Have you published other illustrations? Does your work stand up to professional standards?

If you can answer yes to these questions, then you may have a shot at getting a job as an illustrator. But even so, that doesn't necessarily mean you will be able to illustrate the book you've written. A publisher often views writers and illustrators as two separate people with two separate skills. It pairs up illustrators and writers according to the publisher's vision for the book—not yours. Unless you are determined to become an illustrator of children's books and are able to separate that desire from that of writing children's books, it's better that you don't spend great amounts of time illustrating the book you have written. In most cases, it will be a waste of time and will lessen your chances of being considered for publication.

You will have to convince the publishing company that you are the best artist for the job and will be in competition with several other professional illustrators. What makes you stand apart from the rest?

If you still believe you are the best person to illustrate your book, browse through a variety of children's books from those publishers that may potentially publish your book and pay close attention to the illustrations. How does your artwork compare to these published illustrations? While these artists certainly have their own individual styles, they may also have a common quality that may have been imposed by the publisher. Can you pinpoint what that quality is? Will you be able to alter your style to fit in with the style of the publishing company?

Aside from meeting a specific publishing company's needs, does your artwork suit children's books in general? For instance, consider whether you are able to capture exactly what is needed to move the story along. Do your drawings have too much action taking place or not enough? Will your work appeal to children? Would you be able to illustrate a book other than your own? Keep in mind, if you choose to submit artwork to accompany your text, that you will need to convince the publisher of your skill as an illustrator separate from that of a writer.

## Presenting Your Work

If you decide that you are quite capable of producing professional illustrations and want to take a shot at illustrating a children's book (whether it be your own or another author's), then you need to present your work in a professional manner to increase your chances of acceptance. There are a couple of different ways you can go about this.

### Petition the Editor

If you want to illustrate your own book, you may decide to send samples of your artwork along with the manuscript to an editor. Let the editor know in the cover letter that you are interested in illustrating your own book. You will probably want to include both color and black-and-white sketches to show your range of ability.

You can also create a dummy book to send in to an editor. A dummy is a mock-up of a real book. Be sure to create the correct number of pages (for instance, allow thirty-two pages for a picture book) and leave room for the front matter. Break up the text from the manuscript and paste it on the appropriate pages. This will also help you, as a writer, to see if your text flows well from page to page and if you have too much text or too little text.

### Helpful Hints

Remember, these are just samples. Don't overload the editor with your work, but on the other hand, don't shortchange yourself by sending a limited range. Of course you will want to present your best work, but do not illustrate the entire book at this time.

Once you have the text pasted onto the dummy, it is time to add the illustrations. You should prepare a couple of finished pieces to show your ability as an illustrator. For the rest of the book, use almost-finished sketches to represent the remaining illustrations. Keep a copy of the dummy for your files.

A dummy not only shows your ability as an illustrator, but it also shows that you understand very well the concept and design of a picture book. However, keep in mind that you should submit a dummy only if you are confident that you have the ability to be both a writer and an illustrator. You certainly don't want an editor's opinion of your artwork to be less than first-rate, as it may adversely affect the editor's impression of your writing.

### Contact the Art Director

If you have a burning desire to illustrate children's books, you should send samples to the art director. The art director is normally the person who decides who will be added to the illustrator roster. As a professional illustrator, you should have a portfolio available should the art director want to see more of your work.

Submitting artwork to a publishing house requires just as much research as does submitting a manuscript. Spend a lot of time with current children's books. Can you distinguish traits that are specific to individual publishing companies? Can you tell what it is that they are looking for in an illustrator? Choose to contact publishing companies that produce picture books in line with your style of illustration.

When sending in samples of your artwork, make sure you have the correct contact name, send along a self-addressed stamped envelope, include a cover letter, and above all, follow the publishing company's submission guidelines! If you want to become an illustrator of children's books, you need to distinguish yourself as an illustrator, not just an author who happens to be able to draw. The best way to do this is to approach the art department in a professional manner and present your very best work, leaving the author side of you at home.

## Publisher's Choice

If you don't have the ability to illustrate your story, then who will illustrate it for you? Because the illustrations are very important to your children's book, you want to know that they will be a perfect match. Maybe you have a good friend who likes to draw and just know that the two of you will be able to work together to create an awesome picture book. Or perhaps you are considering hiring a professional illustrator to make sure the work is of the highest quality. Stop right there. Even though it may seem logical—after all, your book will need pictures, and who better than the author will know what needs to be drawn?—you should not submit illustrations with your work. Submitting art (that is not yours) to an editor screams out "amateur" and will adversely affect the way the editor views your writing.

In most cases, the publisher hires the illustrator. Sometimes a publishing company will have a select group of artists who are used consistently to maintain a house style. Other times, a publishing company will hire artists on a book-by-book basis depending on what style fits well with what book. You, as the writer, are not likely to be included in the choice of illustrator. This is something you will just have to accept. But take heart, publishers are in the business of creating and selling books, so they know what they're doing.

Even though the illustrations are an integral part of your story, try to think of illustrating as just another process your book needs to go through to reach the end result. You wouldn't want the responsibility of choosing the printer, would you? Trust the expertise and experience of the publishing company to produce the best results. It is the company's job to recognize what sells and to make its books (and yours) stand up to and surpass the competition.

Once your manuscript leaves your hands, it will be open to interpretation by others. An illustrator's vision may differ from yours, as may an editor's. If you want to be successful in the field of children's publishing, you will open yourself to the opinions of these professionals.

You may just be pleasantly surprised with the results, even though the pictures stray quite a distance from what you originally imagined.

Also keep in mind that if you create a fuss about not having any say in the choice of illustrator, it is likely that an editor will find you difficult to work with and think twice before hiring you for another book. Publishing is a business and in order to be successful, you need to recognize that a team effort is required to sell a book. If you are a good team player and trust in the abilities of the professionals, you will be able to relax and find enjoyment in watching your book reach the hands of children.

Remember that regardless of who illustrates the book and what the pictures look like, the story is still yours.

# Chapter 8

# Submitting Your Manuscript . . . and Dealing with the Aftermath

Preparing the manuscript for submission is not difficult, but it is important. Basically, you just want the manuscript to look clean and professional. Under no circumstances should you turn in a handwritten work. Type it. If you don't have a computer, borrow a friend's or go to the library.

## Preparing Your Manuscript

The manuscript should be double-spaced with one-inch margins on all sides. Use an easy-to-read font such as Courier or Times New Roman. Also, make sure the font is black. This is not the time or place to show off your computer skills. Keep italics and bold to a minimum and use them only if absolutely necessary.

Add consecutive page numbers either at the bottom or top right-hand corner of the page. Do not start a new sequence with new chapters: follow it all the way through.

Print the manuscript on white paper; refrain from using bright colors to bring attention to your manuscript. The paper should be good quality, not the flimsy computer paper that is easily torn. Your manuscript will likely pass through several hands and you don't want the final (and probably most important!) person to miss sections or have difficulty reading it.

Last, but not least, even if the manuscript is on your computer's hard drive, make a copy for your files. Never send your only copy to an editor! That is just a disaster waiting to happen.

## Picture-Book and Early-Reader Layout

If you are submitting a picture book or early reader, do not submit your manuscript in book form (unless, of course, you are a professional illustrator). In other words, do not break up the text by starting a new page where you think it would be appropriate. If you know exactly where the text should be broken, you may add a line break, but keep in mind that an editor may not agree with you. If you aren't sure, don't bother breaking the text—children's book editors are quite capable of figuring it out on their own.

Place your name, address, and telephone number in the upper left-hand corner of the first page, single-spaced. In the upper right-hand corner, place the approximate word count. Center your story's working title about one-third of the way down the page. Skip a couple of lines and begin your story. Because these books normally do not have a lot of text, it wouldn't look right to have a separate title page.

## Chapter, Middle-Grade, and Young-Adult Books

If you are submitting a chapter, middle-grade, or young-adult book, you should follow the basic guidelines from the previous section unless the publisher has its own specific guidelines. However, you may also want to add a title page to make it look more attractive. Just as you would do with picture books and early readers, place your name, address, and telephone number in the upper left-hand corner of the title page, single-spaced. Place the approximate word count in the upper right-hand corner. Type your working title in all caps almost halfway down the page. Type your byline just a couple of lines beneath the title—this could be your real name or pen name, whatever you want to be published under.

On the next page, begin your story. Center the chapter title down a couple of lines from the top, and begin your text a couple of lines beneath that. For each new chapter, start a new page. Number your manuscript pages beginning with the first page of the first chapter; do not number the title page. Again, number the pages consecutively and do not begin a new sequence with new chapters.

### Package Appearance

You will want to create a submission packet with the appearance of professionalism and quality. Do not bind your manuscript using staples, a three-ring binder, glue, or string. Editors prefer to have loose-leaf submissions. If you absolutely must hold your manuscript together in some way, then use a large rubber band.

Now that you have your manuscript ready to go, you are almost there. You also need to include a cover letter (we will discuss this later in the chapter) and a self-addressed stamped envelope for a response and the return of your manuscript. Although you already have your own copy of the manuscript, still enclose enough postage to get it returned. This shows that you care about your manuscript.

If your packet is just a few pages long, as most picture-book and early-reader submissions are, you can use a regular business-size envelope for the submission. Anything more than a few pages long should be sent in a standard manila envelope. You can either print out address labels or handwrite the mailing address very neatly. Don't bother sending the packet express delivery. You will have to wait quite a while to get a response anyway, so there's no point in spending the extra money. Just send it first class through the U.S. mail.

# Submission Guidelines and Deadlines

Always, always, always follow submission guidelines specific to individual publishing companies! You should have this information already, having thoroughly researched the publishing companies on your list. However, if for some reason you don't have this information, get it now. Don't just wing it.

While there are several publishing companies that accept unsolicited manuscripts, don't assume that all do. This should be the first thing you check if you are handling the submission process yourself. By sending in an inappropriate submission packet, you are only wasting your time as well as the publisher's. If you have a burning desire to get your book published by a company that does not accept unsolicited manuscripts, then you may want to consider getting an agent.

It is unlikely that "we accept unsolicited manuscripts" will be the extent of a publishing company's submission guidelines. Often you will find other requirements concerning issues such as multiple submissions (discussed later in this chapter), sample material versus full manuscript, query letters, mailing address, envelopes, formatting and layout, illustrations, and confirmation postcards. Of course, the requirements vary from publisher to publisher, so some may cover more issues than those we've mentioned, while others may not cover any. Just to give you an idea, let's take a look at an example of what one publishing company may request.

## Guideline Dos

There are several things submission guidelines will tell you to do.

For example, let's say you have found a publishing company's submission guidelines posted on its Web site. This company does accept unsolicited manuscripts, but it has separate guidelines for different categories of books. First of all, the company details what type of books are accepted and what subject matters it is looking for in each category. Your picture-book fits in with the company's needs, so you can continue with the guidelines.

The guidelines specify that you should send in a completed picture-book text, along with a cover letter; a query letter is not needed. You are told to submit it on 8½ x 11 plain white paper, loose leaf. The manuscript should be typed and double-spaced. Include your name, address, and telephone number on both the cover letter and the manuscript itself.

Include a self-addressed stamped envelope (SASE) with sufficient postage for the return of your manuscript (otherwise it will be thrown out). Send the manuscript via U.S. mail in a manila 9 x 12 envelope to the address provided by the publisher.

## Helpful Hints

If you forget or decide to forgo the inclusion of a SASE, your likely fate is that of no response at all. If a publisher does not want to publish your manuscript, what makes you think they will go out of their way to put together a rejection packet for you?

See, it isn't so difficult to follow the guideline dos. Though this is just an example, several publishing companies have guidelines similar to these. Of course, publishers will sometimes also include guideline don'ts and these should be followed just as stringently as the dos.

### Guideline Don'ts

Using the example of submission guidelines from the previous section, let's add to them with specifications for what you should not do. This publishing company does want to see completed picture-book text but states that you should not send in illustrations to accompany it. (Illustrations have their own set of submission guidelines outlined on its Web site.) Do not submit your only copy of the manuscript—the company is not responsible for lost material.

Do not send the manuscript via fax, e-mail, or computer disk. The company does not accept handwritten manuscripts, and these will be returned only if a SASE is enclosed. Do not send in bound books or manuscripts laid out in book form. Also, do not include a confirmation postcard, as these are often lost in the shuffle.

While this is just an example, it should give you an idea of what to expect from a publishing company's guidelines. Remember to follow the guidelines to a tee. Any negligence on your part could result in your manuscript being returned with a rejection letter—or no response at all.

## Cover Letters and Query Letters—Know the Difference

The cover letter is very important to your submission packet. The cover letter is what the editor will read first and can determine whether the editor actually reads the manuscript or simply returns it with a polite rejection letter. Like the manuscript, your cover letter should have a clean and professional appearance. Keep in mind that you must make a good first impression.

### Elements of a Cover Letter

The cover letter should be set up as a standard business letter. If you have letterhead, use it. If not, start the letter with your name and address, followed by the date and the publisher's name and address. Beneath this should be your salutation and then the body of the letter. Finally, add the closing with your signature and your name printed beneath the signature. Some also add a note at the bottom telling what is enclosed.

The body of the letter is very important. You want to keep it brief and to the point. Do not go beyond one page (if your manuscript needs that much explanation, you may want to go back and revise some more). State that you are enclosing your manuscript and give the working title. Give a brief description of your book without going into much detail. You want to entice the editor to read the book, not give a full summary.

You may also include a statement regarding how your book would fit in well with the publisher's list. It is always a good idea to include something that shows you have done your homework and are familiar with the company's work.

## Helpful Hints

Include relevant background information about yourself such as any published works, credentials, or expertise on the topic you have written about. If you have none of these, certainly do not say so or apologize for it. Instead you may choose to include a personal experience or reason you wrote the book.

You should never state that your family and friends—or neighbor, mail carrier, hair stylist—thought that this was the best book ever written. Stay away from judging your own book. Obviously you believe it is quality stuff or you wouldn't have sent it. Allow the editor to make up his or her own mind.

### What's in a Name?

Of course, it's always best if you have the name of an editor to send your manuscript to. This is the only way to ensure that it finds its way to his or her desk. Lists of publishing companies will include contact names and titles. However, you should call the company and verify that the particular person still holds that position and double-check the spelling of his or her name. Editors are constantly changing companies, and you don't want to send your manuscript to someone who isn't there. Although the manuscript will either be given to another editor or end up in the slush pile, this shows that you haven't done your homework and doesn't leave a very good impression.

You can also keep an eye on industry news through trade periodicals and market guides. Often you will find information about who is leaving such-and-such company and where he or she is going next.

If you don't have a contact name already, you can always call the publishing company and ask the operator for the name and title of the appropriate editor. As many large publishing companies have several different divisions, make sure you specify that you want the children's book division.

Often, the submission guidelines given by publishing companies will ask you to mail your submission to a generic name or simply a department.

### Query Letters and Proposals

If you have written a nonfiction work, chances are publishers' submission guidelines will request that you send in a query letter or proposal before the editor will agree to read the full-length manuscript. If an editor is not satisfied with a query letter or proposal, he or she will not ask to see your manuscript. However, keep in mind that even if an editor does ask to see the full manuscript, this does not mean you have sold a book—but it does mean you've passed the first test.

### Query Letters

Basically, a query letter is a letter asking an editor if he or she would be interested in seeing your work. Sounds easy enough. However, some writers find this to be the most difficult phase of the entire publishing process. Considering this letter is your one shot at getting your foot in the door, you can see why it can be a little nerve-racking.

A query letter, like a cover letter, should be set up as a standard business letter. Place your name and address at the top, followed by the date and then the publisher's name and address. Open the letter with an appropriate salutation—do not begin with "Hi Mr. Hardworking

Editor!"; "Dear Editor" will work just fine if you do not have a contact name. Following the closing, sign your name and print your name beneath the signature.

The body of the letter should make the editor want to read your manuscript. While this is certainly a sales pitch, don't make it sound so with exclamations of excellence and superiority. State the working title and what type of book you have written. Give a brief, but intriguing, description of the book. You also should provide market research and explain how your book will stand out from those currently available on the same topic. If you can give a reason your book would fit in well with the particular publisher's list, add this too.

Provide relevant background information about yourself, such as why you are qualified to write this book. Also note any other works you have published that are appropriate to the book you wish to submit. If you have any credentials or expertise in the book's subject matter, certainly mention them as well. If you have none of the above, a human interest story or personal experience always works well to add some flavor.

### Proposals

Proposals are what fall between a full-length manuscript submission and a query letter. Normally, proposals are requested for works of nonfiction. While writers have been known to sell books on the proposal alone, it's best that you have a completed manuscript before submitting a proposal, especially for the first-time writer.

A proposal includes sample chapters of your manuscript, a cover letter, an outline, and a self-addressed stamped envelope. The cover letter should be very similar to a cover letter submitted with a full-length manuscript. Again, keep it brief and professional. The self-addressed stamped envelope is self-explanatory. In fact, it should be an automatic response in sending anything to a publisher.

You will also need to provide an outline of your entire manuscript. Normally, this is somewhat similar to a table of contents.

Divide your outline into chapters and then either give a brief description or list the topics that will be discussed for each chapter—if your work is nonfiction. (If you are submitting a proposal for a lengthy novel, then your outline should be replaced by a book synopsis.)

A proposal also includes sample chapters of your work. Check the publisher's submission guidelines for specifications. This gives you the opportunity to back up your fantastic book idea with your superb writing skills. Make sure the chapters you submit are clean and put forward your best work.

## Tracking Submissions

You will need to keep track of your submissions—especially if you choose to send multiple submissions—for several reasons. First of all, it is just good to know where your manuscript is. By noting the date you sent it, you can keep track of how long it stays with a particular publisher. Second, if your manuscript has been declined several times, you don't want to make the mistake of sending it to a publisher that has already seen it. And finally, when your manuscript is accepted by a publisher, you will want to let the other publishers that are considering your manuscript know that they need not consider it any longer.

You'll need to set up an organizational system that works best for you. You may decide that you want to use an index card for publishers you have sent the manuscript to and then arrange them alphabetically for easy access. Or maybe you are a computer buff and choose to set up a spreadsheet tracking system on your computer. Or you could just use a notebook that you leave on your desk and jot down notes to yourself about the submission process for your manuscript.

Regardless of how you decide to set up your tracking system, there are certain things that you will need to include: title, type of submission (query letter, proposal, full-length manuscript), publisher's name, editor's name (if you have a specific contact name), date sent, date returned, and any comments that accompany the returned manuscript. You may also choose to add information that pertains to the submission. For instance, if you sent along a confirmation postcard, you may want to note the date the editor received the manuscript. Or maybe you decide to send follow-up letters or make phone calls and want to note these as well.

Once you get involved in the submission process, you will be able to design an organizational system that suits your needs. In the meantime, consider using the following table to get started.

| Your Manuscript's Title Here | | | |
|---|---|---|---|
| Publisher | Date Sent | Date Returned | Comments |

As mentioned earlier, editors are very busy people and might take quite a while to get around to reading your manuscript. First-time writers who are not aware of this can become panicked and think their manuscripts have been lost. Some will even call or send numerous letters, harassing the editor only a few days after the manuscript was sent.

You, of course, will want to conduct yourself in a professional manner, and therefore take into consideration an editor's busy schedule. You have settled down to a long wait, however nerve-racking it may be. But when is it time to say when and pull your manuscript from a publisher that is taking way too long to review it? It is recommended that you allow a publisher three months with your manuscript. If you have not heard from the publisher by the end of the three months, you can either request the return of your manuscript from the publisher or send a brief letter inquiring about the status of your manuscript.

Of course, the decision is entirely up to you. You are the only one who can gauge how long your heart can take the excruciating wait. But do keep this in mind: Those who are patient usually have a better shot at getting published.

# Roll with the Punches

If you receive your manuscript returned with a rejection letter, don't give up writing altogether. Even some of the world's best writers received a series of rejection letters before finally finding a publisher willing to take a chance on them. Had they given up writing, we would not have all the great literature available to us today.

As stated before, you must have patience and perseverance to be successful in writing. This is especially true after receiving a rejection letter. You have to learn to roll with the punches and not let one person's opinion get you down. Evaluate the response and move on. Time spent feeling sorry for yourself and temporarily giving up is time you can spend improving your manuscript or researching another publisher to send it to.

The world of children's writing is very competitive and can sometimes seem to be a survival-of-the-fittest situation. You need to find your place here, and the only way you can do that is to be strong and confident. That said, you need to know how to cope with responses—either of rejection or acceptance—and best deal with the situation at hand.

## Taking Rejection Personally

Let's say you want a puppy. Being the humanitarian you are, you choose to save one from the pound. As you are walking down the corridor, you notice some really scruffy, disease-ridden dogs; some okay-but-not-terrific dogs, and some that your gut instinct tells you would be perfect. Unfortunately, your apartment has only enough room for one small dog. How do you choose?

You would probably first rule out the disease-ridden dogs. Then you'd pass on the okay dogs, not because there is something wrong with them, but because they just don't strike your fancy. Then you would gather more information about the remaining dogs to help narrow down your choice. Editors face the same sorts of decisions every day. They aren't declining your manuscript to hurt your feelings or because it stinks (unless of course it truly does). They have to make a decision based on the publisher's needs and their own gut instinct.

The last thing you want to do is consider a rejection letter a personal insult. There could be twenty reasons an editor has turned down your work—and none of them may have a thing to do with your writing skills. If you are lucky, you may get a handwritten rejection letter explaining why your book does not meet the needs of the company, but quite often you will just receive a form letter that says your manuscript is not suitable for its list.

Stop yourself if you are considering contacting the editor and demanding a good reason for the rejection of your manuscript. This will only serve to give you a reputation as being difficult to work with, not to mention alienate that particular editor. Business is business, and if an editor does not believe he or she can sell your book, then you'll just have to get over it and move on.

### Using Rejection as Motivation

Some writers find that they simply can't separate emotion from rejection; therefore, they channel that emotion into a motivation tool. Don't laugh; it works. Let's say you receive a couple of rejection letters for a manuscript you know is good. You can either use those rejections as an excuse to give up, which will get you absolutely nowhere, or you could use the rejections to encourage you to improve upon your manuscript and prove those editors wrong. Obviously the latter is the better choice.

Some writers have been known to wallpaper their writing area with rejection letters. When they sit down to write, they are faced with rejection but are determined to beat it. Fueling your determination will help you set aside the feelings of discouragement and bring everything you have to the project you are working on. With hard work, determination, and perseverance you will meet your goals. And if the rejection letters serve to encourage you in that direction, then you actually have those editors to thank for helping you along the difficult path.

## Degrees of Rejection

Not all rejection letters are the same, but almost all are polite. If you are afraid an editor is going to tell you that your work is absolute rubbish and that you should never consider writing again, don't be. Even if your manuscript does stink worse than a compost heap, an editor is not likely to tell you that. He or she will simply decline it with a polite letter.

On the other end of the spectrum, your manuscript may be good quality stuff that the editor has thoroughly enjoyed reading but must decline because it doesn't fit in with the style of books they publish, they have already published a book on that topic, or other such business-related reasons. Again, you will receive a polite letter, but there may be a little more added to this one.

Just as there are degrees of quality in manuscripts, there are degrees of rejection. Knowing this will help you to better evaluate the responses you receive and to take the appropriate next step.

### The Form Letter

The third-degree burn of rejection is structured as a form letter. This is the most common form of rejection. Publishing companies typically have a standard letter that will say something along the lines of "Thank you for your submission, but your book does not meet our needs." The letter is likely to be photocopied and not even include your name, rather "Dear Author." It may not even be signed by a specific editor, maybe just "Editorial Department" or "Submissions Coordinator."

## Helpful Hints

A big mistake you can make is to call the publisher that rejected you with a form letter and ask for specifics. See the list of reasons most companies send form letters, and try to understand that this impersonal approach is not a knock at you, but instead a reflection of the busyness an editor experiences.

Because this is a form letter, you won't get a specific reason your manuscript does not meet the company's needs. This doesn't necessarily mean that your manuscript was horrible. There could be several reasons you received a form letter, including the following.

- Your book did not fit in well with the types of books the publisher includes on its list.
- The publisher has already published a book on the same topic as yours.
- The first person to read your manuscript worked an eighty-hour week and glazed over your manuscript (it never made it to the editor's desk).
- The editor didn't understand the point you were making.
- The editor has a deep-rooted fear of snakes and printed the form letter at the first mention of snakes in your story.

You just really never know with a form letter. The only thing you can be sure of is that your manuscript is not going to be published by that company. The best advice to take is just to move on.

### Personalized Comments

The second-degree burn of rejection comes in the form of a standard letter with additional comments specific to your book. While it doesn't seem like much, a letter that refers specifically to the problems with your manuscript is worth its weight in gold. This means that an editor was interested enough in your manuscript to take the time, even if it is the smallest amount, to write a letter to you.

This is special treatment. Think about how easy it would be for an editor to push the print key and stuff your return envelope with a form letter, or even have someone else do it for that matter. Instead, the editor knows he or she isn't buying your book but wants to give you a little advice anyway. Read over this carefully. Are the comments something you can use to improve your manuscript before sending it off to another publisher? Pay attention to this type of rejection letter and take away from it a learning experience.

### Edited Manuscript

The first-degree burn of rejection includes a standard letter as well as an edited manuscript. This rarely occurs, but some editors have been known to be so passionate about literature that sometimes they just can't help themselves. If you are one of the very lucky few to get such a treat, you absolutely must consider what the editor has done with your manuscript.

Toss aside the feeling of rejection and take notice of the kindness your manuscript was shown. While the publisher may not buy your book, the editor obviously sees some potential. This can be one of the greatest forms of encouragement you may ever see for your book—and all from a rejection letter. Now, keep in mind this doesn't happen all too often, so don't expect it. But if you do happen to receive this type of rejection, know what you are holding in your hands.

## Oh, Happy Day!

We've dealt plenty with rejections, let's now move on to the good news—acceptance. That day will come when you hear the phone ring, debate on whether or not you should answer it, cringe while picking up the receiver because you are sure it's either a salesperson or your mother-in-law, and then hear that sweet voice telling you your dreams have come true. Your family rushes to your side as you swoon and hit the floor in a faint. No, you haven't won the lottery. You've sold your first book!

### The Initial Reaction

Yes, you can't breathe. Yes, the excitement is churning in your stomach. Yes, you feel like you could scream until there's nothing left of your voice. But the editor is still on the phone waiting for your response. Don't worry, editors have come to expect the outbursts of excitement, so if you happen to let out a high-pitched squeal leaving the poor editor half-deaf in one ear, it's okay. But do try to remain as calm as possible, at least until you get off the phone.

You should listen carefully to what the editor says next. The editor will probably explain a little about the process and what you can expect in the following days, weeks, and months. If you have the presence of mind to comprehend what the editor's saying, great. If not, just take notes and worry about them later. You will, however, want to know when you can expect a confirmation letter. If the editor doesn't mention this, you should.

After you have conducted yourself as professionally as possible, immediately call all friends and family members to relay the awesome news. Plan a celebration or just let them come to you. You can either start celebrating that very second, or wait a little bit until you have the other formalities out of the way. While you certainly shouldn't have a pessimistic view, some writers can't completely rest easy until they have signed the contract. Of course, the choice is yours, but know that you will probably have to wait a little while until you receive a copy of the contract, so if you're in a partying mood, by all means get down to it.

### Dos and Do Not's of Celebrating Your Book

- Do have fun.
- Do be proud of your accomplishment.
- Do call yourself an author.

- Do accept compliments gracefully.
- Do not call the editors who sent you rejection letters and gloat.
- Do not go on a shopping spree buying all your family and friends expensive presents (your advance will not cover this).
- Do not worry about what happens next—contracts, royalty statements, new projects, etc.
- Do not drunk-dial an old flame to let him or her know what he or she is missing out on.

That about covers it. Now go celebrate!

## What Comes Next?

After the celebration has died down and the guests have all gone home, you may be lying awake in bed wondering what happens next. Do you need to find a lawyer or agent? What if the deal falls through? After all, you don't have anything in writing, only a telephone call from the editor. How long will it take for your book to reach the bookshelves? Does the book need more work? Who will illustrate the book? The questions could go on and on during the wee hours of the morning when nothing is certain.

While we will discuss contracts and the processes your book will go through in the next few chapters, let's take a look at what you can expect shortly after you receive the news that your book has been accepted by a publisher.

### Confirmation Letter

You will probably first receive a letter confirming that the publisher wants to publish your book and stating that a contract will follow shortly. Or the letter may state that you need to make a few revisions before the publisher can offer a contract. (Your editor most likely gave you this information during the congratulatory phone call.) If you are a first-time writer, it is common practice for an editor to want to see revisions before the contract stage. If you are asked to do revisions, then you will be given a deadline to complete them.

## Contract

Once you receive the contract, you may want to hire a lawyer or a literary agent to review it for you. Contracts can be very confusing to someone who doesn't deal with such things on a daily basis. While publishers aren't out there to cheat you, it is always best to know what you're signing. The contract will detail most of what you need to know about your book and business dealings. We'll discuss contracts in greater detail in the next chapter.

## Monies

Of course, you can also expect to be paid for your hard work. If you are paid royalties, then you will probably get an advance, which is a set amount of money paid to you before the book earns money. You will be paid royalties only once the advance earns out. In other words, the book must earn enough money to cover your advance payment before you can begin collecting royalty checks. Another form of payment is the flat fee. This is one agreed-upon lump sum that the publisher pays you for the rights to your book. You will not be paid royalties or any other monies, regardless of how well your book sells.

## Helpful Hints

Never, ever hesitate to ask for clarification or amendments to your contract, as long as they are reasonable. Your publisher should have no problem clearing up any part of the contract that you aren't clear on. You're better off feeling silly for asking than signing something that you do not understand!

The money you are paid for your book will not have taxes taken out of it. You must pay the taxes yourself. You may want to consult a financial adviser for the best way to do this. But for right now, keep in mind that the full sum you receive is not entirely dispensable; you will need to put some of it aside for taxes.

## Take a Deep Breath

While there is certainly a lot to learn about the publishing business, you have time. Don't feel as though you have to know everything up front. Your editor will work with you. Your fellow writers will work with you. Your lawyer or literary agent will work with you. And of course, you have this book to help you learn.

Don't panic. You've been waiting a long time to get your book published. Just think about all you have learned so far. Apparently you did a great job or you wouldn't have received that congratulatory phone call. You will learn as you work your way through the maze. Everything will be a new experience and a lesson learned. Arm yourself with basic knowledge and then learn by doing.

# Chapter 9

# Know Your Rights Before You Write

While receiving a contract is very exciting, it can also be overwhelming. There is a lot of legal language and complicated publishing terms and phrases. You may decide to hire someone to negotiate for you, but it is important to understand the basics yourself. This chapter will help you learn contract basics and understand some of the writer's rights.

## An Overview of Contracts

Just as publishers are different, so are their contracts. Some will be only a page and others could be forty pages long. While it would be impossible to go into detail about individual contracts, we will discuss some of the elements that are commonly found in them. Having a basic understanding of these elements will help you make sense of these sometimes complicated and lengthy legal documents.

### The Author's Duties and Rights

Most contracts will include a description of the work, and you are expected to fulfill this description. This can include the type of work (fiction, nonfiction), format of manuscript, number of pages or word count, and an outline. Of course, there may be other elements included in the description, but that is up to the publisher. There will also be a deadline date given by which you must turn in the completed manuscript. Sometimes contracts will also include deadlines for revisions or other such work to the manuscript. The contract can describe how the manuscript is to be delivered on the deadline date, such as in hard copy or on disk.

The contract will require that you promise not to include any libelous statements about a third party. You are also required to promise that the work is entirely yours and not copied or taken from another source.

## Helpful Hints

Many publishing companies have technology that can detect plagiarism and outside sources. Play it safe and cite anything that is not yours, and make your publisher aware of it. If not, your contract could be terminated.

If you do include material from another source, you must include a citation and provide written permission, which will sometimes involve the payment of a fee to the party that owns the rights to the material. Most publishers will stipulate that you are responsible for this fee. In regard to some children's books, such as how-to books, the contract may require that you have not included anything that may harm the reader.

The copyright should be in your name, unless you have agreed to a work-for-hire, in which case the publishing company will most likely have the copyright in its name. Also look for the reversion of rights clause, which stipulates what happens to the rights once a book goes out of print or if the publishing company goes under.

### The Publisher's Duties and Rights

The contract will stipulate what the company will pay you for an advance and royalties, as well as what percentage you will take for the sale of subsidiary rights. It will state how many copies of the book you are to receive free of charge, and what price you will pay for additional copies, which is normally at a discounted rate. Or, if this is a work-for-hire, the contract will state the flat fee you are to be paid.

The contract will spell out the handling of rights and what should happen if any rights are sold. Normally, the publisher handles the selling of rights and you are entitled to a percentage of the sale. We will discuss subsidiary rights in further detail in a moment.

Sometimes you will find an option clause in the contract. This clause states that you are required to send your next work to the publisher. The publisher is given the right to first refusal. In other words, you must submit your next work to this publisher and no other until the publisher has declined the manuscript. There are usually no set limits on the time the publisher has to review your next work. So, under contract, your manuscript could be with that publisher for several months before the editor gets to it if there is not a time limit stipulated, while you are stuck waiting for a response, unable to submit it elsewhere.

This is just an overview of common contract elements. The following sections will go into greater detail about those that tend to create the most confusion.

## Understanding Royalties

Once you receive a contract, you will probably first flip ahead to the page that states how much you will be paid. After all, you have put a lot of hard work into this manuscript, and though you are pleased it will be turned into book form, you want to know what your compensation will be. Though your editor has most likely already discussed this with you, it is just a good feeling to see it in writing.

There are two basic types of compensation: flat fee and royalty basis. As mentioned before, the flat fee is given in cases of a work-for-hire. This is pretty straightforward: You are paid a set amount of money for writing a book and turning over all rights to the book; the publishing company normally copyrights the book in its name. You do not receive any further payments.

On the other hand, if you signed a contract to receive royalties, then you will receive royalty statements detailing what monies you are entitled to. It will show how your book is selling and the royalty percentage agreed upon in the contract. Check these statements carefully to be sure you are getting what you deserve. While a publishing company is not likely to cheat you, mistakes can be made. Also keep in mind that while you may have earned the money several months earlier, the check may take a while to get to you. Normally, publishing companies cut checks twice a year, some annually.

### The Advance

The advance is just what it sounds like—an advance on the money you will earn from the sales of your book. Let's say you have written a middle-grade novel. The contract states that you will be given an advance of $4,000 for this manuscript, half to be paid on signing of the contract and the other half to be paid when the manuscript has been received and deemed acceptable (acceptable meaning that you have fulfilled your contractual obligations).

This isn't free money. This is money you would be entitled to once your book is published and begins selling. Your book must earn back the advance before you can begin collecting royalties on it. In other words, your novel must earn $4,000 in royalties before you get any more money.

## Helpful Hints

Your advance is not something you should immediately blow on frivolities and living the high life of a writer. This is money that has to tide you over until your second payment comes, and needs to fund your writing. Be smart!

## Royalty Calculations

Royalties are traditionally paid on the list price (retail price) of the book, or the price you would pay as a customer buying the book. Some companies do, however, pay royalties based on the net price, or the amount of money the publisher is paid for the book (net price takes into consideration discounts that are often offered to buyers, which can come down to as low as half the retail price).

Let's say your middle-grade novel will earn royalties based on the list price. To keep things simple, we'll say that your novel's retail price is $10. Your contract states that you will receive a 10 percent royalty on hardcover editions. So, for this example, you would receive $1 per hardcover book sold. Now, you need to figure in the advance:

Before you will receive any more money, your book must sell 4,000 copies. Beginning with copy number 4,001, you will begin receiving $1 per book sold.

To make this even more complicated, paperback editions of hardcover books normally have a smaller royalty even though the text is exactly the same. Publishers have to do this because the retail price for paperbacks is cheaper, but the costs to produce the book are still high.

Let's say the contract states that you will receive a 6 percent royalty on the paperback edition of your book. So if the paperback edition of your book sold for $5, then you will receive 30 cents per book sold. In this example, you would not need to calculate in the advance since the hardcover edition already earned out the advance.

## Subsidiary Rights

Subsidiary rights is a general term used to refer to all rights to a manuscript other than the initial publication rights. You're probably wondering, what else is there? Well, there's a lot and that's why it's important that you understand what is outlined in the contract regarding subsidiary rights—who has the authority to sell these rights and what percentage of the sale you will get.

How many times have you seen a movie that was based on a book? This falls under the subsidiary rights clause in your contract. Remember, this is your creation. If others want to profit off it, then you are entitled to a cut. In addition to movie rights, subsidiary rights include:

- Foreign language translations (as well as foreign countries that also speak English)
- Television, radio, and theater—any type of performance art
- First serial (publication in periodicals before the book is published)
- Second serial (publication in periodicals after the book is published)
- Book clubs
- Book fairs
- Anthologies
- Textbooks
- Large-print editions
- Audio versions (books on tape)
- Electronic
- Merchandising (any consumer product that is based on your story or characters, such as a stuffed animal or game)

These should be pretty self-explanatory. If you are unsure of what these rights may or may not include, be sure to ask.

If you have an agent, the agent will most likely negotiate the contract to keep some of the rights with the agency. The agent will then work to sell these rights—of course, taking a 15 percent commission.

If you do not have an agent, your best bet is to allow the publishing company to sell these rights. You really don't have direct access to the market or the know-how unless you do this for a living. And if a production studio wants to make a movie out of your book, it will go to the publisher first. You might as well allow the publisher the burden of selling so you can get back to writing.

Usually a publishing company has an entire staff or at least one employee who handles subsidiary rights exclusively. So don't worry, the rights are in good hands. After all, the publishing company wants to make as much money off you as it possibly can.

While each publishing company is different, normally you can expect to split the income from the sale of rights with the publisher 50/50. Again, if your book has been illustrated, you will have to split the 50 percent with the illustrator, leaving you with 25 percent.

## Copyright 101

Some first-time writers are concerned that someone will steal their story and publish it as their own. For this reason, they often apply for a copyright through the U.S. Copyright Office before sending in the manuscript. While it may sound like a great idea, it is unnecessary. In fact, editors who see the copyright symbol (©) on a submitted manuscript will likely deem the writer an amateur. You certainly don't want to come across as unprofessional.

So, how do you protect your work? Simply write it down. That's the beauty of the copyright law. Once you have put your idea into tangible or "fixed" form, in this case on paper in written form, the work is automatically protected under law. Copyright protects both published and unpublished works. You needn't go through the hassle of contacting the office, requesting the needed materials, and filling out the appropriate forms. Once your manuscript has been accepted by a publishing company, the company will do that for you.

### Ideas Are Not Protected

On the other hand, someone could steal your idea (that is, if you haven't already written the story). Ideas are not protected under copyright law. If they were, there would be very few books ever published. For instance, let's say you have an idea for a story in which the protagonist braves a fierce thunderstorm and miraculously pulls through. As your idea, it may seem like something no one has ever published before—taking into consideration specific details, characterizations, and settings.

However, take the idea to its very foundation—human versus nature—and then think of all the books published with that same idea in mind. See, it's really not that original. It is how you present the idea and tell the story that makes your work unique and therefore able to be protected.

### How Long Does the Protection Last?

Not to interrupt your huge sigh of relief, but copyright does not protect your work forever. The U.S. Copyright Office states on its Web site (*www.loc.gov/copyright*) that a work "created on or after January 1, 1978, is automatically protected from the moment of its creation and is ordinarily given a term enduring for the author's life plus an additional seventy years after the author's death." So what happens to your work once it is no longer protected by copyright? It enters public domain.

### What Is Public Domain?

Once a work is no longer protected by copyright, it passes into public domain. This means that anyone can use the work in whatever way he or she wants without having to pay for permission to use it. The author and the author's heirs do not receive any type of payment for its use.

### Helpful Hints

Public domain may mean that you do not have to pay for permission to use a work, but it does not mean you can plagiarize. Just because a work is no longer protected under copyright, that does not mean you can take those thoughts and pass them off as your own.

For instance, think about all the reproductions of Edgar Allan Poe's work. His works have taken form in textbooks, books of individual stories, compilations of his selected works, anthologies, and movies. Because his work is in the public domain, publishers, movie producers, editors of anthologies, and so forth can use his material to make a nice profit. They are paying only production costs because they do not have to pay the author for the right to use the work.

You aren't a publisher or movie producer, so how can you use the works in the public domain to your advantage? Well, you could use a work that is in public domain and add a new twist to it, narrate it from a different character's point of view, provide a sequel to the story, or adapt it into a modern version.

Perhaps you have read a story, and while thoroughly enjoying it, questioned several of its ingredients. Maybe these questions have haunted you so you make an attempt to answer them in your own style. The beginnings of your own fantastic tale are indebted to the original work. You may choose to go into depth about the main character's childhood, perhaps explaining some of his actions in the original story. Or maybe you continue the story onward into the character's adulthood.

Maybe as a child, you read a classic tale only to sympathize with the antagonist. Don't laugh; it's happened. You could re-create the story shedding light on the antagonist's feelings, and turn the story around to make the original antagonist the protagonist.

The possibilities are endless. But if you are considering using a work that is in the public domain to your advantage, you need to see who else out there has had the same idea. For example, if you were fascinated with the wolf from The Three Little Pigs and want to tell his version of the story, you will soon find that this has already been done in *The True Story of the 3 Little Pigs* by Jon Scieszka.

## Plagiarism and Permissions

Now that you know what is and isn't protected by copyright, we'll talk a little about the in-between stuff. In some cases, you will be able to use someone else's work even though it is copyrighted. There are two ways to do this: the legal way and the illegal way.

### Plagiarism

The illegal way to use someone else's work is to plagiarize. Plagiarism is taking someone else's words or ideas and passing them off as your own. Under no circumstances should you ever plagiarize, regardless of how sure you are that you won't get caught. Even if you use material that falls under fair use, you must always cite the source. Otherwise, it is plagiarism.

Plagiarism is considered literary theft and taken very seriously. Always check with your editor if you are concerned about your use of someone else's work. Some things may seem as though they are up for grabs, such as material on Web sites, but they usually aren't. To be completely on the safe side, create an original work and don't rely on the words of others.

### Permissions

If the material you want to include does not fall under fair use, then you will need to be granted permission for the use of the material. For instance, let's say you are writing a nonfiction piece on breast cancer. You have discovered a wonderful article published in a well-known and respected scientific journal that you wish to quote. The excerpt you want to use is straightforward and clearly written—and two paragraphs long. In this case, you would want to get permission to use the excerpt in your book.

You would have to pay for the use of the excerpt and get the permission in writing. Often publishing companies will require a copy of the permission to keep in your file if you are using excerpted material. In fact, the contract will sometimes have a clause involving permissions and who is responsible for acquiring and paying for them (yes, this usually falls to the author).

Also be sure to give credit where credit is due. If you are copying the material word for word, use quotation marks. And always cite your source.

# Chapter 10

# The Editorial Process

After your manuscript has been submitted and accepted, it may be quite a while before you see it again. Many writers don't understand the process manuscripts must go through before becoming a bound book. This chapter will guide you through the first stage: the editorial process.

## The Major Types of Initial Editing

Even though your manuscript has been accepted, and sometimes even after you sign the contract, you will need to do revisions. The book will not be printed as is. Your acquisitions editor may make several general suggestions about the manuscript during the first read-through. After you have made the necessary changes, your manuscript will be read again and likely you'll be asked to make even more changes.

On one hand, you certainly want to listen to the advice and suggestions your editor makes for revisions. After all, this is the editor's job. The editor is paid for his or her experience and expertise, so don't be afraid to use the editor's knowledge to benefit your manuscript. You do want to create quality work that sells well, don't you?

On the other hand, you need to keep in mind that this is your story. Do not scramble to make every little revision suggested before even looking at what you are changing. Carefully consider each change before making it. If the change helps to better your manuscript and you agree with it, then by all means make it. However, if the change takes away from the point you have striven to make or is simply a matter of opinion that isn't important to the overall quality of the work, you can refuse to make the change. Do try, however, to figure out why the editor suggested the change; perhaps an entirely different change can help clear up confusion.

In children's publishing, it is often the acquisitions editor who leads you through the first few stages of editing. Depending on what type of book you have written and how the publishing company is staffed, your manuscript may pass through not only the acquisitions editor's hands, but also the developmental editor's hands for revisions. Regardless of who does the actual editing, there are two different types of editing completed in this first phase.

### Structural or Developmental Editing

If you recall, you put your manuscript through three different stages of revision. During the first read-through, you looked at the manuscript as a whole and focused on structure and content. This is called structural, or developmental, editing and is the first phase of editing the publisher will put your manuscript through.

Basically, the developmental editor will check the organization and consistency of the manuscript. For instance, let's say your manuscript begins with the first two chapters giving background information about the characters and establishing the setting in great detail. The developmental editor may decide that the story would work better if you cut these chapters and began instead with the third, which is where the action begins to take place. The editor may ask you to integrate some of the information from the two chapters throughout the first half of the manuscript, and delete completely the rest of the information because it may not be essential to the storyline.

## Helpful Hints

Again, you must remember to take criticism well. If an editor tells you that a certain part of your book does not fit and should be cut or replaced, swallow your pride and try to understand why the change was suggested. These people read and produce books for a living; they know what they are doing!

This is just one example of what a developmental editor may do. He or she will also look for consistency in character descriptions, flesh out any confusing parts of the manuscript, watch for tense or point-of-view changes, check the breakdown of chapters, and view the manuscript in terms of the "big picture." The editor will usually write an editorial letter to the author addressing any issues, asking questions, and making suggestions. The revision is then left up to the author.

### Line Editing

Once the author turns in a revised manuscript that meets the developmental editor's needs, the manuscript then goes through a line edit. This is equivalent to the second read-through edit you conducted in Chapter 5. While structural editing views the manuscript as a whole, line editing views it line by line. This is where the nitty-gritty work begins.

The editor will be looking at individual lines or sentences to see how well they are structured on their own and in conjunction with the surrounding sentences. The editor will probably first consider whether the sentence has any unnecessary words, whether it is too long or too short, and if it is clear and concise. Are the words carefully chosen and appropriate, and does it use an active instead of passive voice? The editor will then read the sentences surrounding it. Do they all flow smoothly together? Is there a rhythm to their flow, or are they choppy? Does the sentence relate to the others in a sensible and logical way or does it stand out on its own?

The editor will probably make suggestions for revision directly on the hard copy of the manuscript or by using the track changes feature on the computer. The editor may include an editorial letter with the manuscript if there are global changes that need to be made or if there is something needing detailed explanation. But for the most part, the author will be working off the actual manuscript, rather than from an editorial letter, because the changes made during line editing are normally smaller and more succinct than those made during structural editing.

### Copyediting

Next in the lineup is the copyeditor. The copyeditor does the same thing you did during the third read-through, but he or she does this for a living and is much more proficient at it. The copyeditor checks grammar, punctuation, and spelling, and makes sure the text corresponds with the house style.

While your acquisitions editor may have done both structural and line editing, he or she will not do copyediting. Copyediting requires a completely different mindset from the other two types of editing. A copyeditor must be detail-oriented and able to focus on one word at a time as well as the whole. It is a very meticulous job that requires loads of patience. While it may not seem like much fun to you, copyeditors enjoy the responsibility of their job and will certainly let you know where the manuscript does not measure up to their high standards.

A publishing company usually has a copy chief who traffics the manuscripts through to the copyeditors. While a company may have copyeditors on staff, many hire freelance copyeditors as well. Because every manuscript the company publishes must go through copyediting, this process can sometimes take several weeks to complete.

## Helpful Hints

It is highly unlikely that you will have any contact with the copyeditor; you probably won't even know this editor's name. Remember, your primary connection with the publishing company lies with the acquisitions editor; contact him or her. When the manuscript has been copyedited and is ready for your review, usually the acquisitions editor will be the one to send it to you, though this is not always the case.

As in line editing, the copyeditor will mark changes directly on the manuscript instead of describing necessary changes in letter form as in structural editing. (Or if the editing is done electronically, the track changes feature will be used. If you are not sure how to use or read the track changes feature, ask your editor about it.) You will be asked to review the changes made by the copyeditor. Often the changes are simply corrections of grammar, punctuation, and spelling. However, sometimes a copyeditor will revise phrases or query the author about sections that are not clear or about inconsistencies in the text. If you disagree with a change or do not understand a query, talk to your acquisitions editor about it.

The copyeditor is most likely going to be the last person who edits your text. This is also the last time that you will be able to make changes to the text without it costing you. Carefully peruse a copyedited manuscript and make sure that it meets your approval.

## Just the Facts

If you have written a nonfiction book, chances are an additional step will be thrown into the editing process. Most publishing companies choose to put nonfiction books through fact checking or a technical review to verify the accuracy of the text.

This isn't meant to insult you. Obviously the publisher trusts in your abilities or it wouldn't have hired you to write the book. Everyone needs a little peace of mind, so an extra pair of eyes never hurt a manuscript.

A publishing company can choose to send the manuscript to either a fact checker or a technical reviewer. While these may sound like the same thing, there is a slight difference between the two.

## Fact Checking

Fact checking is the process of doubting the accuracy of all facts within a manuscript and checking each and every one. Copyeditors usually make for great fact checkers. They already are tuned in to minute details and can pick up on the smallest inconsistency.

Some publishing companies will ask a copyeditor to fact-check the manuscript while copyediting, though this can sometimes leave room for mistakes. If a copyeditor has to check not only grammar, style, punctuation, and spelling, but also facts, it could get a little overwhelming. A manuscript always benefits from a fresh pair of eyes, so publishing companies will sometimes send the manuscript to a separate copyeditor for the sole purpose of fact checking.

The fact checker will rely heavily on your sources and have a few sources of his or her own. He or she will mark inconsistencies or false accounts and correct them. You will be sent the completed manuscript and asked to make the necessary changes, just as you would for a copyedited manuscript.

For shorter children's books, fact checking will not take much time, even though it is a process of singling out every fact and checking it before moving on to the next. However, for longer children's books, this would become very time-consuming and therefore expensive. In these cases, the publisher may choose to send the manuscript to a technical reviewer instead.

## Technical Review

The technical review is still a form of fact checking, but it does not go through the tedious process of checking each and every individual fact, nor is the manuscript checked by a copyeditor or someone else who does this sort of thing for a living. Instead, a manuscript undergoing a technical review will be sent to a specialist on the particular subject matter of the book.

Let's say you have written a lengthy book about caring for horses. It is likely that the publisher would try to hire an equine vet or even a stable manager to review the manuscript. Or perhaps you have written a how-to book on playing the piano. A publisher would then seek out a professional pianist or piano instructor to give the book a technical review.

The technical reviewer won't check every fact for accuracy. Rather he or she will read the manuscript as a whole and rely on his or her expertise to flag any inaccuracies. Again, the technical reviewer will probably highlight the inaccuracy and correct the problem right on the manuscript. The author would then make the necessary changes.

## Proofreading: The Last Line of Defense

Although proofreaders don't enter the scene until the book has already been typeset, we'll include them here since they are dealing directly with the text and are part of the editorial group. The proofreader's job is to check the set of proofs (which is the typeset book) to make sure that all corrections have found their way into this stage.

The proofreader checks the proofs against the copyedited manuscript for any errors made by the typesetter, such as a repeated paragraph or omitted words. He or she then sends the corrected set back to the copy chief.

During the proofreading stage, you will receive your own set of proofs. This is the very last stage during which you can make corrections. However, keep your changes to a minimum. The author is usually allowed a small percentage of corrections to be made at no charge, but going above that percentage will cost you, since it costs the publisher to make changes. You will be given a deadline to get in your corrected proofs. Do not miss this deadline. If the acquisitions editor does not receive your returned set, he or she will assume the proofs are to your liking and you won't be able to make changes later.

When you return the proofs to your acquisitions editor, your changes will be added to the master set, along with the proofreader's corrections, and sent back for correction. Your changes will be marked with "AA," which stands for author alteration. If you have made more changes than allowed, you will be charged for these additional corrections and the amount will likely be deducted from your first royalty statement.

## Elements of a Book and Design

The editorial team (and you!) has worked its magic, and the text is all ready to go. Now you need to kick back, relax, and wait for the bound book to arrive on your doorstep. But how does the edited text actually become a book? This section will take you through the production process.

### Elements of a Book

Before we actually meet the production team and watch them slowly turn text into a bound book, you need to understand fully all the elements of a book so you can better appreciate all the thought and hard work that goes into each completed product. Let's start with the inside and work our way out.

### Front Matter

Grab the handiest children's book and open it up. What you will usually see first is the other side of the front cover with paper pasted down on it and a blank page. Sometimes publishers will decorate these with illustrations, colored paper, or just keep them blank.

Now turn the page. This next spread (two facing pages) will usually have a blank verso (left-hand page). The recto (right-hand page) is the title page. The title page includes—you guessed it—the title of the book, the author's name, the illustrator's name, and the publisher's name.

When you turn the page, you'll see the copyright page (verso). This page includes important information such as who holds the copyright to the book and the illustrations, the copyright dates, the name and address of the publisher, where the book was printed, the publishing history of the book, the ISBN, and the Library of Congress Cataloging-in-Publication Data. The copyright page may also include other information such as acknowledgments of permissions or a disclaimer.

## Helpful Hints

In your dedication and acknowledgments, try to avoid thanking everyone you have ever met in your entire life. This takes up valuable space and shortchanges the people you really should thank. Be as brief and heartfelt as possible.

The publisher may also have separate pages for a dedication, acknowledgments, preface, or foreword, or the publisher may choose to combine some of these elements onto one page. If the book has chapters, a table of contents will be included in the front matter.

### The Body

You are already aware of all the sweat and tears it takes to create the text of a book, so we won't put you through that again. But your story isn't the only thing that makes up the inside of the book.

Following the front matter is the text, usually on a recto. If the book has chapters, a chapter title or number (or both) will begin the text. Each chapter normally starts on a new page. Some publishers open each new chapter on a right-hand page, and others start a new chapter on whichever page comes next. Some publishers decide to begin the chapter at the top of the page, while others begin halfway down the page.

If the book doesn't have chapters, the publisher will sometimes add a drop cap to the first letter of the text. The drop cap makes that first letter larger than the rest of the text and sometimes takes up two lines or more in height. Or the publisher may just choose to start the text right away without any fancy elements.

The body of the book will likely have page numbers. It may also include running heads or feet. A running head (or foot) is the information that is printed across the top (or bottom) of each page of the body. The running head or foot may include the author's name, the title of the book, the title or number of the chapter, or a combination of these. Chapter opening pages can sometimes lack page numbers, running heads, or feet.

Several decisions have to be made about the text itself, but we'll get to that in a moment.

### Back Matter

The back matter follows the body of the text. The back matter could include a number of things; however, depending on the type of book you have written, it may not have anything. Some common elements of back matter include: appendix, index, glossary, colophon (information about the production of the book, such as the name of the designer or what medium the illustrator used), and bibliography.

Following the back matter information, the very last spread will often copy that of the very first spread with the same design or color of paper used. And that's it! As you can see, a lot goes into the innards of a book. Now let's take a look at the outside.

### The Look

The outside of a book requires a lot of planning. While it may not seem like much—just front cover, back cover, and spine—this could very well be one of the most complicated elements of the book. The cover is what people are going to see first. If they don't like the looks of the cover, chances are they won't bother finding out what's inside. The cover is one of the primary selling tools of the book. It must be perfect.

A jacket will cover the hardcover, adding extra protection. For the prices we pay for hardcovers, we certainly should get a little more. The front of the jacket will have a design that identifies the book, the title, the author's name, the illustrator's name, and mention of any awards the book may have won. The flaps of the jacket will contain promotional copy, usually giving a brief description of the plot and sometimes the author's bio. The back of the jacket will include the ISBN, bar code, and price, and sometimes the publisher's name. You will occasionally find some promotional copy such as quotes of praise the book has received.

Paperback covers include the same information you find on a hardcover's jacket, but it's printed directly on the cover. If a publishing company prints a paperback edition following a hardcover edition, the covers of these two books may or may not be the same.

### The Art of Design

Now that you know what all the elements in a book are, let's discuss how the book comes together to incorporate those elements. The art director has already worked up a schedule for the books coming up far in advance. He or she has assigned a designer to each book and will oversee their work. Sometimes a publishing company will have its own team of designers and equipment for the layout; others will freelance this work out on a contract basis.

### The Designer's Job

First of all, the designer must know the trim size and page count for the book. This will tell the designer how much room he or she has to work with. The designer will then experiment with margin and gutter widths, fonts and their sizes, and leading (pronounced LED-ING; the amount of space between lines) to make the text fit in the allotted number of pages. All these components will either increase or decrease the amount of space the text takes up. The designer must also take into consideration the target age group. Early readers, as you know, will have a lot of white space on the page. Young adult books will have smaller type and little white space.

The designer must decide on the display fonts as well, such as for chapter titles. Speaking of chapter titles, the designer must decide how far down the page the chapter title will be placed and then how far from the chapter title the text will begin. The designer must decide where to place page numbers and where to place running heads or feet (right, left, or center).

A designer also has the responsibility of creating a cover design. As already mentioned, the cover design is very important because it influences the buyer's first impression of the book. The designer may create several different cover designs for the same book. Because it is such an important aspect, a meeting will usually be called to get different opinions before a final decision is made.

### Adding Illustrations

If the book has illustrations, whether a picture book with illustrations on each page or a chapter book with scattered illustrations, the art director will hire an illustrator to get the job done. Sometimes the publishing company will have a select list of tried-and-true illustrators to choose from, or sometimes it may decide to try out a new artist.

## Helpful Hints

Regardless, you as the author have very little say in the choice of illustrator. As was said earlier, it's often the publisher's choice. You will have to trust that the publisher knows what it's doing.

The illustrator will go through a process of submitting roughs to the art director to get approval before completing the pieces. Once the art is completed, it will be scanned and then incorporated into the layout. Of course, the designer assigned to your book will play a role in this process.

If the designer is working with a picture book, he or she must decide where the illustration will be placed on the page in conjunction with the text. Look at the various picture books at your disposal. Compare the layouts. Some will have text that runs along the bottom of the page with the illustration taking up the biggest portion of the page. Some will have the text running along the top. Some will place the text within the illustration. And some will use a combination of these. Also look at the sizes of the illustrations. There is a lot of variety in the layout of text with illustrations. All this is usually decided by the designer with input from the art director.

### The Production Manager

The production manager has the important job of making sure your manuscript makes it to tangible book form, and begins plans for your book long before he or she actually receives it, such as selecting a typesetter. Because the production manager oversees all books on any given list, he or she will have scheduled the printing of your book, as well as others, in advance of having it land on his or her desk. Once the production manager does receive it, he or she will send it off to the printer on the appointed date, ensuring a smooth and timely printing schedule.

While this may not seem like such a big job, the production manager has a lot more to do than just coordinate printing schedules. One thing to keep in mind while reading about all the production manager must do is that this person has the added struggle of staying within a set budget for each book. This will heavily influence most of the production manager's decisions and sometimes cause him or her to find creative ways of getting what's needed for the money that's been budgeted.

## Production Goes to Press

One of the major decisions the production manager must make is which printer to select. Usually, the production manager will have a good relationship with several different printers, having worked with them in the past and on a regular basis. If this is the case, the decision may not be too difficult. However, if the budget for a particular book is lower than usual, or if a new printer has caught his or her eye, the production manager will need to do a lot of research about pricing and quality from various printers.

The production manager should be familiar with the capabilities of the printer's equipment and the quality of work it produces. The production manager should also know what the printer's needs are regarding submitted materials and advance scheduling. And, of course, the production manager must know the printing costs.

### Paper Choices

Another major decision a production manager must make is what type of paper to use. While you may think paper is paper, it isn't as simple as that. There are several different kinds of paper a book may be printed on. Take a look at a variety of children's books. Can you feel the differences in quality and texture of the papers used?

For instance, compare a hardcover book to a mass-market book. The hardcover book will usually use acid-free paper, which will ensure its durability for many years. The mass-market book will use a lower-quality paper that will brown after a few years. Obviously, you get what you pay for, and this cost is reflected in the retail price of the book.

Price isn't the only consideration in paper choice. The production manager will also have to decide on the following.

- **Weight.** The weight of paper is determined by how much a standard ream of that particular paper weighs. For instance, 25 lb. paper means that a ream of 500 sheets (25" x 38") of that paper weighs 25 pounds.
- **Bulk.** Bulk is determined by how many sheets of paper make up an inch.

- **Color and finish.** Color and finish affect the overall appearance of the pages.
- **Opacity.** This will determine if the text from the reverse page will show through.

As you can see, the paper alone calls for several decisions to be made. But the production manager's job does not end here. He or she will also have to decide on the type of binding for the book.

### Binding

During the binding process, pages are put together in signatures, usually sewed or glued. A signature is a group of pages normally thirty-two to a group. However, depending on the type of paper used, the press capabilities, and the trim size, a signature could also be sixteen, eight, or even four pages. The signatures are then gathered and bound together, either by sewing or using an adhesive. The cover is then attached to the gathered signatures using an adhesive. If you don't understand this process, don't worry about it. Just know that this is one of the many processes your book must go through to reach its final form.

Binding will affect how well the book opens. For instance, have you ever found yourself straining to keep a mass-market book open while reading? Sometimes it even requires two hands. Then again, the binding for music books often allows those books to open flat without your having to keep them open.

### Going to Press

Once the production manager has made all necessary decisions, the book is then ready to be sent to the printer. Because it includes several minute details and can become a very complex process, we will only briefly describe the printing process. However, most authors find it interesting to learn the basics of what the book has to go through to reach its final form.

### Blues

The printer will create a film from the files provided by the production manager. This film is used to create blueprints, commonly referred to as "blues." The blues represent the book's final form. They are bound pages, but the quality will not be as good as the final product. The blues will be the last chance the publisher has to review the book before it is sent to press. Corrections made at this stage are very costly. However, it is important to double-check the placement of illustrations, make sure that all pages are there and in order, look for unwanted marks on the pages, and confirm that all elements have come together properly.

The publisher will then send the blues back to the printer highlighting any corrections that need to be made. If there are several corrections, the book will need to be typeset again and pages adjusted, starting the process over again. After corrections have been made, the book will go to press.

### Print Run

The production manager specifies the quantity for the print run in the instructions to the printer. The print run is the number of books to be printed. However, this number is rarely exact. Most often, the publisher will have made room in the budget for the printer to print a few extra copies.

The film is then used to set up the press for the print run. The book will be printed on large sheets of paper, the paper will be folded and gathered into signatures, the signatures will be trimmed, and the book will be bound.

### Four-Color Printing

If you have written a picture book that will be printed with full-color illustrations, there is an additional step to be aware of. While the printing process will remain the same, color will need to be added.

This is usually done in a four-step process, hence the name *four-color printing*. The four colors used in this type of printing are cyan, magenta, yellow, and black (commonly referred to as CMYK). The image will go through the printer four times, each time adding a new color. The combination of these four colors will result in the variety of different colors you find on covers, in magazines, and in illustrations.

### The Bound Book

The production process, for an author trying to be so patient, can seem like a lifetime—especially since you will have little if any involvement in the process. As you can see, the book goes through a lot to reach its final form. So if you were wondering why your book was scheduled to come out on a list two years after signing the contract, this is why. However, your book will not immediately reach the bookshelves after it has been bound.

The bound book will be shipped by the printer—or bindery if it was sent elsewhere to be bound—to the publishing company's warehouse. This trip could take anywhere from a couple of weeks to a couple of months, depending on how far the printer is from the warehouse.

A publishing company's warehouse may be down the street from the publisher, or in a different town or even state. This is where the books will be stored until they are sold to buyers. Large publishing companies may even have several warehouses scattered throughout the country.

Once the books arrive, inventory needs to be taken to ensure that the shipment is complete. The warehouse employees will then either get the go-ahead to begin processing orders or be told to hold the books for a while to give the reviewers time to do their thing and bring attention to the book. Advance copies may also be sent to potential buyers as a marketing strategy.

As the author, you will likely receive an advance copy as well. This will be your prized possession, at least until you get another book published! Editors realize how exciting this is for authors and normally don't waste much time getting the bound book in the mail. This advance copy is considered a courtesy, so don't expect your other free copies to be delivered just yet.

# Chapter 11

# Marketing and Publicity

Y ou've spent a great deal of time trying to sell your manuscript to publishers. Now that you have succeeded, how is your publisher going to sell your book to the public? This chapter will guide you through some of the common marketing and publicity tactics used to help promote and sell your book.

## The Catalog

The publisher's catalog is likely to be the first place your book receives any form of attention. Normally, the company will have two lists per year—spring and fall—and it will create a catalog for each list. Your book will be categorized by the pub date, along with all other books that will come out in that same month.

As mentioned earlier, your acquisitions editor will write the catalog copy that will accompany a picture of your book's cover, if available. The book's announcement will also include the trim size, page count, ISBN, author's bio, a brief description of the book including age or reading level, and price, and may mention any marketing plans intended for the book.

Sales reps will be busy trying to sell the books on an upcoming list and will bring a catalog along to their meetings. The catalog is a very useful selling tool, as it contains brief but succinct information a book buyer can use to make a decision.

The sales team does not have the time to sit down and read each book that they sell. Therefore, they will rely on information provided to them by editors and the catalog. The editors will likely have written up tip sheets, which include information about the book and the author (and illustrator if applicable). The editor will then go before the sales team and give his or her own pitch for the books he or she represents. This gives the sales team an opportunity to get their questions answered and get a better feel for the books. Sometimes, they will receive other promotional materials to help back their sales pitches to buyers, but don't expect a whole lot for a first-time author. Normally, a spot in the catalog and a brief pitch from your editor is all the sales team is going to get for your book.

## Helpful Hints

If you do not receive a catalog automatically, call your editor and request one. This will probably be the first instance in which you see your name next to your book in print. It can be very uplifting and satisfying to know that your book is actually going to be sold alongside all the other great titles that made the final cut.

The sales reps aren't the only ones who use the catalogs. A publicist may decide to send out catalogs to reviewers, journalists, and other such contacts to raise awareness and help promote the publisher's latest books. Interested book buyers may request a catalog if they haven't already been contacted by the sales reps. Individuals, such as yourself, conducting research on a particular publisher may also request a catalog to check out the upcoming titles.

## Book Reviews

Most publishing companies will send out review copies of new titles. While it does cost the company shipping charges to send the books, if the book is reviewed in a publication, that's the only cost for the valuable publicity. Often, publishers want their books to be reviewed before the books actually reach the shelves. Therefore, they will send out bound galleys for select titles. These are copies of the typeset book before it has been finished and sent to the printer. Other companies will wait for the book to be printed and send out advance copies before placing the book in stores.

A book review is great publicity and can heavily influence book buyers. Librarians, especially, will rely on book reviews to help make their decisions on what books to purchase for their library system. Reviews are great for public exposure. While consumers will be reading the reviewer's opinion of the book, good or bad, it may pique their interest, swaying them to buy the book and create their own opinion.

A book review seems like the perfect way to bring your book to the attention of all book buyers, from the buyers of major chains to librarians to the general public. However, getting your book reviewed isn't guaranteed. First, you have to make the publisher's cut.

Because sending out books for review does cost money—and though it doesn't seem like much, after you've sent out 500 copies, it can add up quickly—publishers must decide which are going to be worth that money. As stated several times throughout this book, publishing is business. Some publishers will decide to send only those titles that they believe have the best shot at making it big. Some will send only those titles that have well-known authors' or illustrators' names attached to them. As a first-time author, your book may not make this initial cut. However, the only way you'll know is if you ask.

Don't lose heart. Publishers sometimes choose to send most, if not all, their new titles to reviewers, though they may be a little more selective with the reviewers they choose. However, if your book is sent to a reviewer, this doesn't guarantee that a review of your book will actually make it to publication. Once again, you'll have to make the cut.

Reviewers, especially the top reviewers, are sent a good percentage of all new books. Publications have only so much room to use for reviews and come out only every so often. Unfortunately, those books that are chosen for reviews are often tied to a well-known name, whether it be author, illustrator, or publisher. While it seems as though it is exactly these that do not need the extra attention, they are what people want to read about.

On the bright side, there are a few publications that try to review all new books, giving each author a fair chance in this very competitive field. The next section will highlight some of the top publications people seek out for book reviews.

### Where to Look for Reviews

Your publisher will likely send your book to at least one, if not all, of the following, top reviewers. These publications are those that are combed by industry professionals on a regular basis. A favorable review in one or more of these will almost certainly result in increased sales of your book. You are likely familiar with these publications already from your market research. But now that you are published, you will be perusing them for a different purpose:

- *Booklist.* The American Library Association's magazine targets primarily librarians. The magazine reviews more than 2,500 children's books per year.
- *The Horn Book Guide.* A biannual publication that is dedicated to children's literature. It includes reviews on almost all new hardcover titles.
- *Publishers Weekly.* One of the major industry trade publications. Almost all those involved in the book business read it on a regular basis. It has a section devoted to reviews called "Forecasts," with a subsection for children's books.
- *School Library Journal.* This targets primarily librarians and boasts that it reviews more books per year than any other publication.

These publications aren't the only places you'll find reviews, but they are considered the major reviewers.

### Evaluating Your Reviews

If your book does get a review, prepare yourself before reading it. It may not be the spectacular praise you were expecting. Reviewers can sometimes be harsh. If your review is not favorable, just remember that this is one person's opinion. You've made it through several critiques already for this book, what is one more? Sure, some people will decide not to read it, but there are people who may not ever have heard of your book otherwise. Bad publicity is still publicity. The review has achieved public exposure for your book.

On the other hand, if the review is favorable and does dish out that spectacular praise, this is not the time to practice your modesty. Clip it, frame it, show it to everyone you know. Above all else, take pride in the hard work, emotional suffering, determination, and love that you put into your book. Also, you can expect the orders to start rolling in.

## Press Releases

The publicity department may write and send out press releases in addition to advance copies of your book. A press release is a brief news article that newspapers or magazines can include in their publications. Because the publicist has already written it, the editors of these publications can just paste it in and not have to worry about assigning someone to do the research and write the article, making it a convenient form of coverage.

Some publishers may choose to send out press releases to major newspapers and magazines with the hope that the editors will request a copy of the book for review. This saves the publisher the cost of shipping the book when there is no guarantee that the cost will pay out with a published review. Some publishers will send press releases to all major newspapers throughout the country. Others will target only local areas or any area that has a relationship to the book, such as your hometown.

## Media Tie-Ins

The press release will be brief and to the point. The shorter, the better. This is an introduction to your book and will include important general information such as title, author, type of book, and a brief description. Because it is used as a selling tool, the copy will try to grab the reader's attention from the start. While the press release may include pertinent information with only a few hooks thrown in here and there, some publicists brainstorm different angles to help grab the attention of the media as well as the reader.

For instance, if your book's subject ties in to a current media event, this is a perfect angle from which to write the press release copy. Just for fun, let's say that your book is about life on other planets, and the government has recently released a report verifying the existence of intelligent life on Venus. The whole nation is glued to the television and newspapers, and there you are as the author of a book relating to this current event.

The publicist will send out a press release promoting your book in relation to these current findings. The media may snatch it up hungrily, request a copy of your book for review, set up television and radio interviews, and take you all over the nation. Your book will sell big and you will reach fame and fortune as the "Alien Author." If the publicist hadn't sent out these press releases, your book may have sat alongside others gathering dust while everyone forgot about reading in light of the verification of alien existence. While this is an unrealistic example, it does show that press releases can grab the attention of the media if written from a creative angle and tied in to current events.

## Author Participation

The publicist has probably already asked you to fill out an author questionnaire, which asks for information the publicity department can use to help promote your book, such as where you currently live or where you grew up. If you haven't been asked to fill out a questionnaire, you may want to provide the publicity department with this information yourself.

If you know your hometown's newspaper would be interested in doing a spotlight on a local author, give the publicist the newspaper's name and address. Especially if you live in a small town, the publicist might not even be aware that the town has a newspaper. Try to think of any other publications that would be interested to learn about your book. Collecting this information yourself makes it easier on the publicity department and increases your book's chances of getting a wide circulation of press releases.

## Conference Displays and Promotions

Another common and important promotion your book may be considered for is its display at professional conferences. Publishing companies often attend several professional conferences a year. They will have a booth set up to display new releases and perhaps some strong-selling backlist titles. Representatives from the company will be there to work the booths, answer questions, and show off their products. Sometimes authors are invited by the publisher to attend and participate in book signings, though this is usually reserved for bestselling or top-name authors.

There are several conferences that take place throughout the year. You can check with *Publishers Weekly* (*www.publishersweekly.com*) to get a list of conferences and their dates. The two biggest conferences that you'll probably be interested in are the American Library Association's annual conference and BookExpo America (BEA). Both of these draw publishers from all over the country. Attendees can walk around and view the fancy displays, talk to sales reps and editors, acquire an armload of free goodies, and make numerous contacts within the publishing industry.

If your book is displayed here, just think about all the people who will give it a glance, if not further study—authors, illustrators, librarians, booksellers, publishers, editors, sales reps, pretty much anyone involved in the book business. This is an important promotion for your book. Not only will it raise awareness, but it will most likely garner interest in the book, and you as well.

There are also several smaller book fairs, conventions, and conferences that may be of interest to you. Check with your editor to see if the publisher will be setting up shop at any regional conferences. If you can attend, do so. It is an invaluable experience.

### High-Profile Promotions

The most widely known marketing and publicity strategies include author tours, television and radio interviews, and advertised book signings. But don't start packing your bags just yet. These types of promotions are reserved for those authors and books that are top sellers for the company. Sure, if your book receives a literary award or makes it to the bestseller list, you'll have a good shot at your fifteen minutes of fame. However, most books and authors (though they may be top quality with solid selling records) do not reach this level of publicity.

Publicists are not going to send review copies of your book to every talk show—television or radio—they can think of. In the end, this would simply be a waste of time and money. Pay attention to those books you hear about on talk shows. Have you already heard the author's name a thousand times before? Is the subject matter a hot topic in current events? Is the author or illustrator someone who's reached fame and fortune already? For most of the books you hear about, you will be able to answer yes to at least one of these questions.

High-profile promotions cost big bucks. A publisher must be sure to get good returns for the investment. This is why it isn't likely a publisher will choose to take such a risk on a first-time author. Unfortunately, fame is often a Catch-22 deal. No one will pay attention to you unless you are famous, and you can't become famous until someone gives you the needed attention. Of course, there are always the stories of overnight successes. You can hope—just don't bank on it.

If this has shattered your dreams, think about what a hassle it would be. You would be expected to fly across the country to talk to someone who probably hasn't even read your book, leaving your family and responsibilities by the wayside. You would probably suffer some degree of stage fright and run the risk of making a fool of yourself on national television. You would probably have to go through some sort of interview preparation course with your publicist or someone else. You see, fame doesn't come without a price.

If you still have that burning desire to get high-profile promotions for your book, see what you can do without the publisher. The next section will discuss a few things you can do to promote your book and yourself.

## Visit Bookstores and Libraries

Because of limited budgets, your book may not receive the publicity and advertising from the publisher that you believe it deserves. However, you need not rely solely on the publisher to raise awareness of your book. This section will give you a few ideas of how to take the promotion of your book into your own hands.

You want to sell your books, right? Since it is not a good idea to sell books yourself, you may want to begin your promotion campaign by visiting those businesses that do sell your books: bookstores. You probably already know the bookstores in your local area pretty well; you may even know some of the staff. While these are certainly great to start with, don't count out bookstores in nearby cities or towns. You can find bookstores within easy driving distance by doing a search on the Internet. Or if there is a place you visit regularly (a different city or state where your parents live, or a favorite vacation location), consider visiting the bookstores in this area as well.

Create a list of bookstores, and schedule times in your planner to drop by each one and introduce yourself. It's important that you pencil them in—it's very easy to have great intentions and just never get around to doing it. If you are serious about promoting your book, you won't hesitate to schedule related activities.

## Introduce Yourself

You are an author with a book in print; people will want to meet you. But don't assume that you will get oohs and ahhs just by walking into a bookstore. If you aren't a top-selling author with a picture plastered everywhere, chances are no one can tell you apart from the everyday customer.

First, find out if the bookstore has your book in stock. If not, you may want to have a friend or two or several order the book to raise interest. If the book is in stock, be friendly and chat a little with the staff. Introduce yourself and your book. You may find that the staff will open up with information regarding how well your book is selling. However, don't interrogate the staff. If you flat-out ask if your book is selling well, this will put the employee on the spot. Maybe he or she has never even seen your book. Having to admit such a thing will likely make a person feel uncomfortable and want to escape the conversation as soon as possible. Your best bet always is to assume no one knows you or your book.

Becoming chummy with a bookseller may entice him or her to give a little attention to your book, especially if the bookstore is located in your area. This isn't likely to happen with the chain superstores—they expect to be paid for any attention given to a book. However, if you have a cozy independent children's bookstore in your local area, the store manager may very well choose to display your book for a short period, announcing a local author.

### Book Events

If you want to promote your book with an event, such as a book signing, you must first verify that the particular bookstore actually holds such events. Some bookstores only sell books and do not bother with hosting public events. Call the bookstore and ask. Any employee should be able to tell you.

Visit the bookstore and request a copy of its calendar of events. This will tell you what type of events normally take place and give you an idea of how far in advance the bookstore schedules these events. For instance, if the calendar lists events for the next three months, you can bet that you will have to schedule at least three months in advance. Next, you will need to decide what type of event you would like to see take place. This could be anything from a book signing to an author reading to a character party where the kids dress up in costumes pertaining to the book.

When pitching your idea for an event, you should contact either the store manager or the person who arranges community relations activities. When you make the initial call, find out who it is you need to speak with. A part-time employee won't be able to set up an event. Once you have a name, try to speak with that person directly. You may even want to send a letter introducing yourself and describing your idea for an event. Be sure to include the title and ISBN for your book! Also, to increase your chances of a scheduling, offer to help promote the event.

If you are a first-time author, you may find that the bookstore isn't interested in scheduling your event. Don't worry too much about this. Thank the person you spoke to for his or her time and move on to the next bookstore on your list. The first bookstore may have actually done you a small favor. Think about it: If you are an unknown and you schedule a book signing, you may be gravely disappointed to see only two people show up the whole day (aside from the friends who came out of obligation). Such a disappointment could easily discourage you.

If the bookstore doesn't wish to schedule you for an event, or if it doesn't sponsor events at all, you can still promote your book. Offer to sign the copies of your book the store has in stock. Sometimes bookstores set up bins especially for autographed books. Even if they don't, an autograph is likely to persuade a customer to buy your book.

### Visit Libraries

Even though libraries don't sell your book to the public, don't rule them out as a promotion venue. Often children find great books in the library, only to later pester their parents into buying them. And word of mouth can work wonders for the overall sales of a book. Promotion is not just selling; it is also raising awareness and getting your book out there.

Visit the local library. First, see if it even owns a copy of your book. If not, don't stress out, but you may want to donate a copy. The library will be glad to have it and may even place it face out on the shelf or set it out on a display table. Librarians want to bring in people just as much as bookstores do. If they believe a local author, such as you, will help get the public's attention, they will use your book as a hook.

## Public Exposure

If any of your friends own a business, you could beg them to put a copy of your book in the window of their shop. Of course, you shouldn't ask them to try to sell copies; ask them to just put it out for display. People walking down the street will likely stop and wonder what type of book is placed in the window of a butcher's shop, for instance.

You could ask your friends to carry around a copy of your book for a few days so that it can be seen by the public. This may require them to actually hold onto the book while taking a walk through the neighborhood, setting it down next to them on a park bench or on the table at a diner, or leaving it on the dashboard of the car. How many times have you come across an interesting-looking person in the park or on the street and wondered what types of books he or she reads? If someone else is wondering the same thing about your friends, finding a children's book in their possession might interest them even more.

If you really want to get down and dirty, you could always ask your friends to send a copy of the book along with their children to school. Of course, this will work only if the kids like you and don't hate your book. Keep in mind that word of mouth can be just as damaging as it can be helpful. If your friends are parents, they could always check out their kids' school library and ask about your book. You may want to provide them with copies just in case the library doesn't own it. They can donate a copy of your book, thus getting it into the school systems.

## Public Speaking

If you have a fear of public speaking, get over it. One of the best promotional strategies to employ is to speak about your book. If speaking in front of people is a deep-rooted fear, ask your family and friends to help. Practice on them and ask for their feedback. Just think, some day you might land a spot on *Oprah*. You certainly don't want to go into such an interview cold. Get your practice in now and in no time you'll be a pro.

## Interviews

Even if your publicist hasn't set up interviews with local television and radio stations, don't rule them out. With a little work, you could get a short spot to promote your book. Before you run to the phone to set up an interview, you'll really should come up with a hook and put together a press kit.

If you want to get an interviewer's attention and persuade him or her to feature your book, you'll have to give that person something to work with. If your book can be tied into some current event, this is great. Be sure to emphasize this in your press kit. If you can't tie it to a current event, try to dig up some new statistics about your topic. You will need to approach this from an angle that highlights the importance of your book. Get creative and brainstorm. Ask your friends and family for help, and do what you must, but do not simply say, "This is simply the best book ever written."

Once you find your hook, begin putting together a press kit. Your press kit should, at the very least, contain an author bio, a press release, and sample questions for the interview. If you have supplied any of these materials to the publisher, you already have part of your press kit started. If your book has received favorable reviews, include copies of these, too, and if you have scheduled a book event, mention this as well. Include anything you feel would add to your book's importance. Have you already gathered the names and contact information for local television and radio stations? Then you're ready to go.

Send your press kit off to local media outlets. Because you are a local author, you are likely to get at least a little bit of attention. If you plan on spending time elsewhere, target the stations in that area as well. Just be sure to include your dates of availability.

### Speaking at Schools

If you are interested in promoting your book to a group of children, or in some cases teenagers, speaking in schools may appeal to you. Your speech could take many forms, and will take a lot of thought. Because you are speaking directly to children, you will have to capture their interest and attention from the get-go. You will have to make it fun, exciting, interesting, and informative all at the same time.

Think of the events you considered proposing to a library or bookstore. Would any of these work in a school setting? For instance, if you have written a picture book, you may want simply to read it aloud to the group. However, you will probably want to animate your characters through the use of your voice or even act out parts of the story to keep your audience's attention. This would probably work better in a classroom setting than in an auditorium with the entire school as your audience.

## Helpful Hints

If you do decide to speak at a school, this is a great opportunity to get a sense of what your reader thinks of your books. While an adult reviewer might heap praise on your pitch-perfect character development, and a parent might swoon over your role model protagonist, a child might have a small critique that can determine how your next book will be written. Remember that you are writing for children.

If your book is for older children, you may want to read a portion of it and discuss the writing process. You could add in activities that pertain to the story, or give the children short and fun assignments that demonstrate a stage in the writing process. However, be careful that you don't actually use the word *assignment,* or the children may not be very open to the idea. You want this to be a fun experience that covers up the fact that they are actually learning something.

If you are interested in speaking in schools, start with your local school system. Call and speak to the principal. Give a brief description of your idea and see if he or she is interested. If so, you can follow up with your author bio, a copy of the book, or parts of your press kit—something that will give the principal an idea of what you will be presenting. From there you can work with the principal to schedule a date and time, and determine the setting and audience.

## Go the Extra Mile

Of course, you could do all of this and still want to do more. This is where your creative genius comes into play. Brainstorm all possible ways for your book to gain attention. Start with those that aren't so over the top and go from there. Be careful that you don't become so zealous that you drain your bank account. Some promotion strategies can make quite a dent in your checkbook.

Some authors create materials featuring their book and hand them out to anyone who'll take them. For instance, you could design fliers, brochures, or even bookmarks and pass them out yourself or ask a library or bookstore to keep a pile for people to take from. If you are a poster person, you could design a poster and ask friends and family to put up copies in their places of business, or you could post copies on bulletin boards in libraries or other such places where the book would benefit from exposure.

Or you could create a Web site that talks about your book, your background, why you wrote the book, and maybe give advice to aspiring writers. You will probably also want to include your publisher's contact information as well as the ISBN and price for the book. This will allow those who are interested to order your book directly from the publisher without having to hunt it down. Web sites take a lot of time to create and maintain, so be sure that this is something you want to keep up before going to all the trouble.

One thing you do not want to do is stand on a street corner and sell your own books. Traditionally, it is not appropriate for authors to be seen selling their own books. Your contract may restrict you from doing so anyway. Certainly let the world know your book exists, but leave the selling to the booksellers.

# Chapter 12

# The Indeterminable Future of a Children's Book Writer

Throughout this book, you've read over and over how difficult writing and getting published can be. Well, now it's time to put the difficulties aside and focus on what that hard work can do for you. This chapter will introduce you to the awards and recognition you may receive as a children's writer, as well as let you in on the joys of grant money.

## Financial Aid

Did you know that you can get free money to help you establish a writing career? We're not talking about the royalties or flat fee payments you are entitled to after you have been published, but about grant money. Many writers aren't aware of the financial aid they can receive through grant money. Grant money is basically free money given out to help support a cause, in this case children's literature. Grant money does not have to be paid back as does a loan.

There are several different types of grants available for both published and unpublished authors. Some grants are specific to genres, and some cover all genres. Some grants offer a few hundred dollars and some offer a few thousand. Some cover only specific expenses, such as writing supplies, and some can be used for any expenses related to your writing needs, such as child care.

It is quite likely you will find one or several grants you are qualified for and that suit your writing needs, but you need to pursue them. All too often, writers are either unaware of grant opportunities, fail to do the research needed to find the right grant(s), or assume they won't get the grant and simply don't try for it. Because of this, a lot of money is out there for the taking, but not being used.

### Where to Look

If you are interested in researching grants, first check with any writer's organizations you belong to. For instance, the Society of Children's Book Writers and Illustrators offers a General Work-in-Progress grant of $1,500 to the winner and $500 to the runner-up, as well as others that are specific to unpublished authors, young adult novelists, and nonfiction writers. Of course, there are several other writer's organizations out there that offer grants. Start with those of which you are a member, then research all others. You never know; you may just happen upon an organization you haven't heard of before and choose to become a member, with or without the opportunity for a grant.

Your next stop should be your local library. Search its database for books offering grants for children's writing, but don't stop there. You may also be qualified for grants outside the specifics of children's writing. For instance, you could be eligible for grants awarded to minorities or those working within a specific area, such as AIDS awareness. If you have the time and energy, look through all books on grants that the library has to offer.

Your last source should be the Internet. While the Internet offers a wealth of information and is sometimes great for research, if you type in a search for grants, you will likely have to sift through thousands of sites before finding what you want.

## How to Apply

Applying for grants is no easy task. You will need to contact the organization sponsoring the grant for qualifications, guidelines, and application forms. You will usually need to prepare samples of your work to include in the submission. Though it may not sound too difficult (you fill out applications and forms all the time, right?), applying for a grant actually requires a very specific form of writing.

## Helpful Hints

Always read the fine print of grant submission guidelines as well as the fine print of your contract, if you have one. Make sure that your contract would allow you to receive funding, and make sure that the grant extends to writers already under contract.

Your best bet is to research grant writing before diving into it on your own. Though there are writers out there who never apply for grants, there are also those who tap into these opportunities on a regular basis and are familiar with the proper procedures. To have a fighting chance against these individuals, your grant writing skills need to be top-notch. There are several books and guides available that will help you learn the art of grant writing, such as *Finding Funding: The Comprehensive Guide to Grant Writing* by Daniel M. Barber. A number of these will likely be found in your local library.

## The Newbery Medal

So you still have dreams of fame and fortune? Well, you just might get it if you are awarded the Newbery Medal. The Newbery Medal is considered the highest honor a children's book author can receive. Everyone in the children's literature world holds their breath every year waiting for the announcement of the winner.

Winning the Newbery Medal will put your name on the lips of all involved in the industry. Recognition isn't the only reward, though. You will also see a tremendous boost in the sales of your book, since every library, bookseller, and many children and adults will all of a sudden feel the need to own your book. The Newbery Award is not something to be taken lightly.

### History of the Newbery Medal

If you recall, John Newbery was the eighteenth-century bookseller who was responsible for the turning point in children's literature with the publication of *A Little Pretty Pocket Book*. This book combined elements of education and instruction with amusement and entertainment, paving the way for modern children's books. Frederic G. Melcher recognized Newbery's achievement and in 1921 proposed to the American Library Association (ALA) that an award be presented in honor of Newbery. The ALA readily agreed, and thus the first children's book award was born. Ever since then the Association for Library Service to Children, a division of the ALA, awards the Newbery Medal annually to one children's book author.

As the first and most distinguished children's book award in the world, the Newbery Medal carries a lot of weight. The medal's purpose, according to Melcher's agreement with the ALA, is "to encourage original creative work in the field of books for children. To emphasize to the public that contributions to the literature for children deserve similar recognition to poetry, plays, or novels." The Newbery Medal has certainly lived up to its purpose.

### Qualifications and Criteria

Since only one author can win this award per year, there must be qualifications set to help make the difficult decision a bit easier. Those children's books considered must have been published the previous year and authored by a United States citizen or resident. The book must also have been published in the United States. Reprints and compilations are not eligible.

The book can be comprised of any type of writing (fiction, nonfiction, poetry), and the text is primarily what will be taken into consideration. The committee can't take into consideration an author's past works or the author's reputation, nor can the committee take into account how well the book sells or its popularity. The book can't rely on other media and must be a "self-contained entity."

## Helpful Hints

The book's target audience must be any age group of children through the age of fourteen. In other words, an adult book children happen to enjoy is not eligible for consideration.

When deciding on a book's degree of excellence, the committee must take into consideration the interpretation of the theme or concept, the handling of characters and setting, how the plot is developed, overall presentation and organization, and style.

Finding excellence in children's literature is easy; deciding on the "most distinguished American children's book" is not. This was understood from the very beginning, and so the committee is allowed to recognize other books for their merit. These books are called Newbery Honor Books.

## The Caldecott Medal

It was a wonderful day back in 1921 when the Newbery Medal was founded, because the authors of children's books were finally getting the recognition they deserved. This continued on happily until people began to realize that several books reached their quality of excellence through the illustrations. But the illustrators weren't getting the credit they deserved.

### History of the Medal

In 1937, Frederic G. Melcher again went before the American Library Association and proposed that another award be established to honor the artist who created "the most distinguished picture book of the year." This honor would be called the Caldecott Medal, named after the nineteenth-century English illustrator Randolph J. Caldecott. Of course, the board loved the idea.

Every year since, the Association for Library Service to Children has awarded the Caldecott Medal to one illustrator alongside the presentation of the Newbery Medal. These two medals go hand in hand in recognition and stature. All booksellers and libraries will keep copies of the Newbery and Caldecott winners. These books are truly the "most distinguished" children's books for any given year.

## Qualifications and Criteria

This medal, too, has qualifications and criteria that must be met for a book to be considered. Since this medal is also hosted by the ALA, as you can imagine, the criteria are quite similar to those for the Newbery Medal.

The book must have been published in the United States during the previous year and illustrated by a United States citizen or resident. The illustrations must be original work and found in no other source. The book's target audience must be children. Though most picture books are targeted to younger children, the age of the target audience may be through age fourteen. The illustrations must provide a child with a "visual experience," in which the storyline or concept is developed through the series of illustrations.

The committee can't take into consideration an illustrator's past works or the illustrator's reputation, nor can the committee take into account how well the book sells or its popularity. The book can't rely on other media and must be a "self-contained entity." Committee members make their decision based primarily on the illustrations, though other elements (such as the text) can be taken into consideration.

The committee must take into consideration the illustrator's execution of the artistic technique chosen, how well the illustrations act as an interpretation of the text, how well the style complements the storyline or concept, the use of illustration to describe characters and setting, and/or the use of illustration to convey information.

Of course, there are hundreds of excellent illustrators out there. Because only one can be honored with the Caldecott Medal each year, the committee is also allowed to select the work of other artists to be commended as Caldecott Honor Books and give credit where credit is due.

## Keep Writing!

There are several guides out there offering tips for writing. While they may all take different approaches to the craft, they all agree on one thing: You must write to learn to write well. Practice does make perfect.

### Helpful Hints

Go back and review the section on battling writer's block if you feel as if you can't think of a new project. You are full of ideas, and now is the time to start sifting through them for your next book. Also try going through your old notes from your previous manuscript. Something you cut or didn't have time to add may be the inspiration you need!

Regardless of whether you are currently searching for a publisher, conducting market research, or self-promoting, you must continue to write every day. This can't be emphasized enough. It is easy to find excuses and fall into a lull; it's even easier to stay there. But once you begin to feel that burning desire to begin writing again, it can be difficult to get back into the routine. The only way to combat this is to maintain the writing routine, even on those days when you believe you have nothing worthwhile to write.

### Pre-publication

If you have a manuscript in the editorial or production phase of publication, then begin a new project. Not only will it help keep your mind off what is happening to your manuscript, but it will also give you something to talk about when your editor asks about any other work you have to show him or her. If an editor is interested in building a relationship with you, the last thing you want to do is come up empty-handed. Show your editor that writing is important enough to you to work consistently at strengthening your skills.

If you are having difficulty selling a manuscript to a publisher, then you may want to ease your frustration by beginning a new project. Riffle through the idea files and see what strikes your fancy. You certainly should not use the submission process as an excuse to stop writing.

The excitement and frustration involved with a first manuscript can be a major deterrent in your writing routine—if you let it. Just keep in mind that you won't strengthen your writing abilities or successfully sell a manuscript unless you keep writing.

### Post-publication

If you have already published a book, your second (as well as the third and fourth) book will be very important. Let's say your book hasn't sold very well, for whatever reason. Your publisher may not want to sign you up for anything else. Does that mean you're a failure? Of course not. Nor does it mean that you won't be able to sell another book. You just need to find a different publisher. The selling record may have nothing to do with your writing abilities, so you should strive to make your second book even better than the first. You have to prove to future publishers that you are an excellent writer, regardless of the first book's sales figures.

## Helpful Hints

There can be many reasons a book does not sell well. Oftentimes a publisher and an author miss the train on a fad. Something can be all the rage when an author finishes a manuscript, but by the time that manuscript has been made into a book, the fad is over and old news. You obviously cannot control this, so don't beat yourself up—you're still a published author!

Now let's say your book was a top seller for the publishing company. (Of course, in this instance, we'll give you all the credit for the outstanding sales.) While you may think it gets easier from here, the opposite is actually true. Your readers liked what they saw in the first book; now you have to keep their favor with the second. This means that the second book has to be just as good, if not better than the first, or you risk losing your audience for any future books you write.

In either of these scenarios, the temptation to give up can be hard to resist. If you take yourself and your writing seriously, you will do whatever it takes to combat this temptation. The easiest way to do this is to maintain your writing routine. You have the experience gained from a previous book on your side. Use that experience and keep writing. The more you write, the better you will become at the craft.

## Find a New Path

If you have written a picture-book, this doesn't suddenly brand you as a picture-book writer. Now, whether you want to establish yourself as a picture-book writer is a different story. You may receive advice telling you to continue writing picture books until you have established yourself in the industry. On the other hand, you may receive advice telling you to write whatever you want; your enthusiasm for the book will show through in your writing. So what should you do for your next book?

### The Options

Let's say your picture book is currently going through the production process. You have been working on a young adult historical novel. However, a member of your writer's group tells you that you should write another picture book and make a name for yourself before plunging into other areas of children's writing. Because you have already proven your writing abilities to one publisher, it will be easier to do the same with another, if you stay within the same genre. Those who try their hands at writing everything under the sun give off the appearance of being unsure of their abilities and not willing to perfect their work in one area.

While this does make sense to you, another member of the writer's group disagrees and makes you think again. The other member is adamant in her belief that if you write what you want to write, the determination to succeed will show itself in your work. Just because you were successful with a picture book doesn't mean that you can't be successful with a young adult novel. If you force yourself to write a picture book when you want to write something else, your heart won't be in the project, thus negatively affecting your writing abilities. However, if you do write the young adult novel, you will be so determined to prove that you can that you will do whatever it takes to get the manuscript as close to perfect as you can.

### The Decision

The decision isn't an easy one. You want to build a career as a writer, yet you don't want to sacrifice your writing and ideas to the cause. Unfortunately there isn't a right or wrong answer here. You must make the decision on your own.

However, to make the decision-making process a bit easier, you might want to consider your motivations for writing. If you write with the sole intention of getting your work published and into the hands of children, maybe you should follow the first writer's advice. If you write simply for the sake of writing, you should probably go with the second writer's advice.

### Write for Magazines

While this book has focused on the writing and publication of children's books, this isn't the only area open to you if you enjoy writing for children. You may also want to consider writing for magazines. A lot of writers break into book publishing by first adding credits to their names through magazines. Some find it rewarding to write for both books and magazines. And others simply prefer the magazine style.

If you haven't already, check out the different children's magazines available. You'll find that there are hundreds. Some are geared toward a general audience, others are targeted to specific groups, such as girls, preschoolers, boys who like to play hockey, and so on. All sorts of topics are covered in children's magazines. If you have written a piece that doesn't sell to book publishers, consider trying to sell it to a magazine, because it is likely that you will find a magazine that specifically handles your piece's topic.

If you think writing for magazines is for those who can't cut it when it comes to book publishing, think again. Magazines have their own styles and guidelines for written material. If you aren't familiar with writing magazine articles, you'll probably find that it is more difficult than writing books. For one thing, you usually have to write within a specified word count. It can be quite a challenge to find the exact words you need when you have a limit on how many you can use.

Magazines have their own submission guidelines and pay rates. Just as you would follow a book publisher's guidelines to the letter, you should do the same with magazine publishers. Magazines normally pay per word or per article. If you become a proficient magazine writer, you may find that you make a better living through magazine publication than book publication.

## Teach a Class

Although you should never assume you know everything and should always be open to new learning experiences, you may find that you have already learned a lot—enough to teach others. Because many published writers are unable to live solely on the income from their books, most try to find a supplemental source of income in a related field. Those who thrive on social interaction and are confident in their abilities may choose to teach a class.

## A Teacher's Challenge

Teaching requires a lot of hard work and preparation. You must create a syllabus for the entire semester before even the first class. And even though you may think you have developed the perfect schedule, allowing just enough time to cover everything you want, chances are you will have to reevaluate periodically and readjust your course outline. Sometimes the class simply doesn't operate at the pace you determined. You don't want to skim over important parts just to keep up with a schedule, nor do you want to take too long to explain things and allow students to get bored with the topic.

Will your class cover only one type of children's book (such as picture books) or will it give an overview of all? Do you want to touch on children's publishers and how to submit manuscripts? What about the process of book production? The institution may or may not provide some guidelines, but you will undoubtedly need to make some decisions on your own.

How will the class be conducted? Do you want to spend most of the time lecturing, or would you rather have the students write and conduct the class in a way similar to a critique group? Perhaps you would like to use a combination of the two. If you are going to have the students write, what type of books will they be writing? How will you persuade the students to critique each other constructively?

You also need to consider your qualifications. If you don't know the ins and outs of the publishing industry, you probably don't want to cover this in your class. If you've been published, you can speak from personal experience. If you haven't been published, some institutional directors may not think you are qualified enough to teach a class, and even if you do get a teaching position, your students may doubt your instruction. This isn't to say that you can't be a wonderful and informative teacher if not published, but just know that some prejudice may be directed toward you, so have proof of your qualifications ready.

While teaching a class can be very challenging and stressful, it is also a wonderful experience. You are teaching others about a craft you love, inspiring them to become great writers for children, and thus reaching children in an indirect way. You will also discover a lot through your students, making your teaching experience a learning experience as well.

### Finding a Position

A good place to start looking for a teaching position is at a local college or university. Check with the continuing or adult education department to see if it already offers a course on children's writing. If it doesn't—and you are sure you want to do this—tell the department head you would like to start one. He or she should be able to tell you the proper channels you need to go through to get a class started. Of course, not all institutions will want a children's writing course, but it certainly doesn't hurt to ask.

## Helpful Hints

Many colleges and universities have a well-stocked staff, one or more of whom usually specializes in various types of writing. Do not be offended if you are respectfully declined, but ask them to keep you in mind in the future as a visiting lecturer. This creates new contacts and potential opportunities to teach in the future.

## Accept It—You're a Writer!

Before you can go any further, you must accept that you are a writer. This may seem ridiculous, but many writers fail to take themselves seriously. If you can't take yourself seriously, why should a publisher or other members of the writing community do so? This isn't to say that you can't have fun with writing, but you can't consider it just a flight of fancy either.

Having read so far in this book, you understand how much work and dedication writing requires. But since you have read this far, you also haven't been frightened off. We hope this means that you are up to the challenge and have a burning desire to succeed.

### Identifying Yourself as a Writer

Have you gathered ideas for future projects? Have you conducted market research? Do you know who the children's publishers are? Have you set up a writing schedule? Have you taken steps to get your thoughts and ideas down on paper? Have you written a first draft? Have you suffered through the revision process? If you've answered yes, you are a writer.

Many people hesitate to call themselves writers before they are published, or even after they're published for that matter. Once you take on the title, responsibilities suddenly swoop in from dreamland. You actually have to do this. You have to write and find a publisher. You have to devote time and energy to your craft when there are a thousand other things you could be doing. You have to dedicate a portion of your life to children's literature. It can be a scary thing, but it can also be the boost you need to get your motivation and determination to kick in.

If you allow yourself to truly believe you are a writer, not a whole lot will stand in the way of your goals. Love your craft and take pride in your work. Be a children's book writer!

# **Resources**

*An Author's Guide to Children's Book Promotion* by Susan Salzman
Raab.

*A Basic Guide to Writing, Selling, and Promoting Children's Books:
Plus Information about Self-Publishing* by Betsy B. Lee.

*The Business of Writing for Children: An Award-Winning Author's
Tips on How to Write, Sell, and Promote Your Children's Books*
by Aaron Shepard.

*Children's Books and Their Creators* by Anita Silvey (Editor).

*Children's Writer's & Illustrator's Market* by Alice Pope.

*The History of Children's Literature: A Syllabus with Selected Bibliog-
raphies* by Margaret Hodges.

*How to Write a Children's Book and Get It Published* by Barbara
Seuling.

*How to Write and Illustrate Children's Books and Get Them Published*
by Treld Pelkey Bicknell and Felicity Trotman (Consultant
Editors).

*How to Write and Sell Children's Picture Books* by Jean E. Karl.

*It's a Bunny-Eat-Bunny World* by Olga Litowinsky.

*Origins of Story: On Writing for Children* by Barbara Harrison and
Gregory Maguire (Editors).

A *Sense of Wonder: On Reading and Writing Books for Children* by Katherine Paterson.

*Ten Steps to Publishing Children's Books: How to Develop, Revise & Sell All Kinds of Books for Children* by Berthe Amoss and Eric Suben.

*The Way to Write for Children* by Joan Aiken.

*Writer's Handbook 2006* by Barry Turner (Editor).

*Writing Books for Kids and Teens* by Marion Crook.

*Writing Books for Young People* by James Cross Giblin.

*Writing a Children's Book: How to Write for Children and Get Published* by Pamela Cleaver.

*Writing for Children* by Catherine Woolley.

*Writing for Children and Teenagers* by Lee Wyndham.

*Writing with Pictures: How to Write and Illustrate Children's Books* by Uri Shulevitz.

*You Can Write Children's Books* by Tracey E. Dils.

*Young at Heart: The Step-by-Step Way of Writing Children's Stories* by Violet Ramos.

### Web Sites

Booklist: *www.ala.org/booklist*

Bookwire: *www.bookwire.com*

The Children's Literature Web Guide: *www.ucalgary.ca/~dkbrown*

Children's Writer: *www.childrenswriter.com*

The Children's Writing Supersite: *www.write4kids.com*

The Horn Book, Inc.: *www.hbook.com*

Literary Market Place: *www.literarymarketplace.com*

Publishers Weekly: *www.publishersweekly.com*

Purple Crayon: *www.underdown.org*

School Library Journal: *www.slj.com*

Society of Children's Book Writers and Illustrators: *www.scbwi.org*

Writer's Digest: *www.writersdigest.com*

# Index